WE ELECT A PRESIDENT

Here is the full story of the presidential campaign in America. It goes behind the scenes and describes the struggle for power within the political parties to determine who shall win the nomination. The author reveals the obstacles encountered by each man who makes his bid for the presidency, and cites colorful examples from past campaigns to show what tactics and strategies successful candidates have used to woo the electorate. He tells what goes on at the conventions, explains how the electoral college works and thoroughly covers the president's role as the voice of the nation.

BOOKS BY DAVID E. WEINGAST

WE ELECT A PRESIDENT

FRANKLIN D. ROOSEVELT
Man of Destiny

WALTER LIPPMANN
A Study in Personal Journalism

THIS IS COMMUNISM

WE ELECT A PRESIDENT

by DAVID E. WEINGAST

Illustrated
with
Photographs

JULIAN MESSNER, INC. • NEW YORK

Published by Julian Messner, Inc.
8 West 40 Street, New York 18

Published simultaneously in Canada
by The Copp Clark Publishing Co. Limited

© Copyright 1962 by David E. Weingast

Fourth Printing, 1963

Printed in the United States of America

Library of Congress Catalog Card No. 62-11243

To Beatrice and Four

who made room for the donkey and the elephant

CONTENTS

WE ELECT A
PRESIDENT

★ ★ ★ ★ ★

CHAPTER ONE

WHO WANTS
TO BE PRESIDENT?

DOWN THROUGH AMERICAN HISTORY, MANY PEOPLE HAVE asked, "Who wants to be President?" The question betrays what most people think about the Presidency: that it is heavy with responsibility from which there is no escape; that the President, during his four-year term, dwells in the public domain with no chance of a private life; that the Presidency in our time, at least, is the toughest, most bruising job in the world.

Who wants it?

The answer, of course, is that lots of men—and occasionally a few women—want it. They want it badly enough to work for it years in advance of the presidential nominating conventions. They want it enough to spend themselves and their money in a drive to win delegates before the conventions open. They want it enough to travel the length and breadth of the land—Alaska and Hawaii included—in a dogged search for supporters.

A man who's been bitten by the presidential bug tries, by every possible means, to get his name and his face before

11

the public. He wants to look like a winner before the big nominating convention is called to order. He may enter various state primary elections to draw nationwide attention to himself. He will use every stunt, every trick, every gimmick that may speed him to his goal: to be named a presidential candidate. Many of these devices are standard equipment to politicians and include the following:

> shaking hands—on the street, at factory gates, in supermarkets and stores, in door-to-door canvassing
>
> speaking to a crowd—three or more persons—if one can be assembled
>
> praising the local townspeople, especially the local ladies
>
> kissing babies
>
> taking an interest in local exhibitions or achievements, or contests
>
> getting time on radio and television programs to spread the gospel
>
> giving away an assortment of election-time novelties—buttons, hats, stickers, and toys—food and drink
>
> using every form of advertising and publicity—leaflets, posters, billboards, skywriting, balloons, newspapers, telephone, rallies, meetings

By these methods and many others, the would-be President tries to step from the class of political unknown to a serious candidate. The price comes high, but the prize, the Presidency of the United States, makes it worthwhile.

Despite the wear and tear of the Presidency, despite the fact that the job takes a brutal toll of the man in office, there is not and never has been a shortage of men who want to be President. Throughout American history there has always been an abundance of candidates ready to make the sacrifice. For this we should be thankful because our democratic form of government rests on a three-cornered foundation—Executive, Legislative, and Judicial. All three sides—the

President, the lawmaking Congress, and the Federal Courts —are necessary if our government is to operate in the way planned by the Founding Fathers—the men who wrote the Constitution back in 1787. If nobody wanted the responsibility of the Presidency, our democratic system would either fall apart or be changed in ways impossible to predict. Certainly we would find ourselves with a government unpleasantly different from the one we now have.

We must keep this in mind when we get impatient with the behavior of some aspiring candidates. We must remember that there are worse things than the political wars in which prospective candidates demolish each other at regular four-year intervals. Nobody has yet come forward with a good substitute for the free-for-all that finally gives us a single candidate from each of the two major conventions. And nobody has proposed a better way for the two chief candidates to tell the people their story than the present method of campaigning.

Why do we speak of "two chief candidates" when everybody knows there are other candidates, from small parties? Because the voters understand that the real presidential competition is between Democrat and Republican. Several of the small parties have a fairly long history. Others come and go. Some put up a vigorous fight and may rack up a sizeable vote. But practically speaking, the candidate of one of the two major parties is expected to win the Presidency. The role of the smaller parties is discussed in Chapter 3.

The legal requirements for the Presidency are stated simply and briefly in our Constitution:

Age: at least 35 years
Birth: a native-born citizen
Residence: at least fourteen years a resident of the United States

These are qualifications that millions of Americans have

in common. Yet, scholars who have studied and written about the American Presidency claim that in all the United States there are just a few men who are really equipped to run for President. This means that, over and above the legal, Constitutional qualifications for President, there must be other requirements that are important, even though unwritten.

These unwritten qualifications are not necessarily the same today as fifty or a hundred years ago. With changing times come new attitudes and new needs. A candidate in the 1960's or 1970's might have characteristics that would have barred him from the Presidency in earlier years. The candidate of the future may have attributes that would have eliminated him if he were running today.

What are some of the unwritten qualifications of a presidential candidate in our own time? Personality is one.

Though the Constitution says nothing about the personality make-up of presidential candidates, it is clear that the job calls for certain qualities. One of these is ambition. Only a man fired with ambition could ever hope to be President. This is, in fact, a primary ingredient of any presidential candidate. He must really want to hold the number one post in the nation. He must have a strong wish to wield power, for the day a man is sworn in as President he inherits a huge complex of power.

This is a general principle, to which there are exceptions, of course. There have been a few Presidents who were not extremely ambitious men. This small number includes William Howard Taft and Dwight Eisenhower. But the Presidency of the United States in our time carries such responsibility and power that only an ambitious man would be drawn to it.

A man who shrinks from occupying the center of the stage, who gets queasy when all eyes are on him, could not function as President. Our nation's Chief Executive works not only within our borders, but in a world setting. He must be sufficiently tough and durable to deal face to face with other leaders who speak for millions, maybe hundreds of millions, of people.

A man who shuns public exposure, who is uncomfortable with responsibility, or who hates to make decisions—big ones—could not carry the office of President of the United States. The Chief Executive must have exceptional muscle structure, both physical and psychological. Without it he could never stand the rigors of campaigning for office in the first place. He must be able to survive round-the-clock travel, endless hand-pumping, the loss of sleep, an erratic eating schedule, and separation from his family. Once in office he must both lead his nation and go before the world as the sole representative of the dignity, the tradition, the ideals and the power of the United States of America.

The President must be sufficiently thick-skinned to take abuse, to see his words and actions misunderstood and misrepresented, to see himself caricatured by critics and enemies both at home and abroad. He must be hardy, yet flexible. He must be able to mingle easily with the spokesmen of a hundred other nations and cultures. He must be able to deal with rough, ward-level politicians and with fragile intellectuals who may belong to his camp.

As a candidate for the Presidency, or for re-election to the Presidency, he must be able to sight political enemies at a distance and win them over, or neutralize them, or eliminate them.

The presidential aspirant must be a politician. When he seeks the nomination he must be skillful and even ruthless in enticing delegates into his camp, while beating back opponents who may try to raid his own legions. He must know when to hold out the promise of rewards, when to threaten, and when to wield the big stick. He must understand the art of persuasion, because the American political system is based on this art. Legislators have to be persuaded; so does the public. The American President doesn't get things done just because he orders them done. He must, instead, convince people of the merits of his case. He is the nation's most important lecturer and teacher.

The great Presidents have not necessarily been the ones with the highest I.Q.'s or the highest academic degrees, but those who knew how to lead a free people. This kind of leadership requires skill in explaining, in teaching. In a democracy people will go along only if they understand.

A successful President needs more than a brilliant program. He must have the politician's genius to win for it the backing of the lawmakers and the citizens. He cannot make proposals that outrage deep tradition and loyalties. He must be at the head of the nation but not too far ahead. A skillful politician has his finger on the public pulse. He senses how far he can go without losing his followers. He must be able to endure disappointment, broken promises, and sometimes betrayal. He must be prepared to see his record—private and personal as well as public—displayed to the voters. Any youthful blunders or indiscretions are likely to be used against him by his political enemies. If he is highly sensitive and quick to be offended or bruised, presidential politics is not for him. Those who can't stand the heat, Harry Truman once said, should "stay out of the kitchen."

The man who wants to be President must like people because the office demands continuous exposure to people. A great part of his day, every day, is spent with people, official and unofficial. There is a steady flow of people his way, whether he is at the White House or anywhere else. They call to give advice or to seek it; to offer help or to ask relief; to praise, to blame, to vent their anger; to steal a few minutes of his time so they can say they've seen the President. If people irritate or upset him; if crowds disturb or frighten him, he is not cut out for the Presidency. No President can function except in constant relation to people. He must weigh every decision for its immediate and its long-range effects on people—his own people and those of other nations. A President who is out of touch with people—their hopes, their needs, their feelings—must fail in his office.

Another personality trait that marks the serious candidate for President is moderation, even-temperedness, and ability to see both sides of a question. This does not mean that a presidential aspirant must be namby-pamby or a man-sized Little Lord Fauntleroy. We expect our President to be masculine, vigorous, forceful, but we do not want him to be conscienceless or dictatorial. A man who wants to make extreme changes in our political, economic, or social system does not stand a chance of being elected. Ours is a two-party system. While third parties—or even fourth, fifth, or sixth parties—compete for votes, the American people have been generally indifferent to them. Since the days of George Washington there have been two major parties. Even in his time, two main parties had formed around opposing leaders. While these two parties stood for different principles, they both went after wide public support. These early political parties were the ancestors of our present-day Republican and Democratic organizations. Both groups have always tried to win the approval of most Americans. Though they have often had distinctive programs, they have tried at the same time to attract voters from all regions and from all economic and social classes. The two major parties have tried to avoid being exclusively the spokesmen for any one class or any single part of the country.

The broad appeal made by the two major parties means that the candidates they put forward must have a fairly generous view. The candidates must be tolerant men who see the Presidency in relation to the United States as a whole. They cannot go before the country as the champions of any one group or section. If they do, they are sure to fail.

The United States is a huge country with a big range of features. Every candidate, as he travels around the country, is constantly reminded that

> its geography includes extremes of temperature, topography, rainfall, and climate
>
> its industry is varied, productive, and inventive
>
> its agriculture is abundant to the point of surplus
>
> its economy—its businesses, its factories, large and small—is privately owned and operated for profit. No large group, not even the lower paid, unskilled workers, want to change to any other economic system such as communism or socialism
>
> its people are middle class in their thinking. A few are millionaires and some are very poor. But the nation as a whole follows a middle-class pattern of life
>
> its basic tradition, deeply rooted, is that the United States is a democracy. Our government answers to the people and to the people only. They freely vote approval or disapproval of the government's record of achievement. Neither a king, nor a dictator, nor a clique of bosses does the people's thinking for them. Most Americans believe that our democratic system can work better. But greater democracy must come through gradual, peaceful means—through education and the ballot box. Neither sudden change nor violence can be part of the program of improving our democracy.

A candidate who asks for votes in such a country must have before him this picture of the United States. He must satisfy a majority of the people that he is not a dangerous man, or a fanatic, or an extremist, or a violent man. He must convince the voters that as President he will work within the tradition of American democracy; that he will not try to do by force what must be done by persuasion. He must appear before the nation as a man who will not use the presidential office to wage war against his private or public enemies. We expect our President to be above this, to be a man of dignified, quiet strength. Up to the present, at least, the American people have been willing to vote only for candidates who were reasonably tolerant, flexible, and moderate in their views.

Some writers of American history books, especially European authors, think that American Presidents are pretty sure to be weak-willed, wishy-washy types. They seem to think that our requirements rule out the chance of getting a really strong, able, two-fisted President. These authors argue that a man of force and power and strong beliefs could never clear all the hurdles in the competition that finally gives the United States a President. American history gives little support to this point of view. In spite of our requirements, the caliber of men who have won the Presidency compares favorably with world leaders generally.

So much for personality. There are other presidential qualifications that aren't mentioned in the Constitution. Let's look at some of these additional unwritten requirements of the Presidency. They, too, are important in determining which hopefuls can make a serious try for the Presidency.

Chapter Two

WHO STANDS A CHANCE?

In addition to certain qualities of personality that have already been discussed, any serious bidder for the Presidency must also offer a combination of other characteristics. A candidate does not project himself before the nation just because he wants to be President. He must first satisfy the leaders of his party that he has what it takes. Sometimes the "what" seems unfair. A man from Mississippi, for example, would have a hard time making political headway as a Democratic party candidate because Mississippi is a sure Democratic state. The leaders of the party would have little interest in a candidate from such a "safe" state, even though he were an able man. They consider Mississippi in the bag for the Democratic party. As they see it, the party has nothing to gain by putting up such a candidate. They'd prefer someone who could carry a big but uncertain state along with him. They assume, of course, that a candidate will have magnetic appeal in his own state and will pull a majority of votes his way. This means that a man coming from New York, Ohio, Illinois, Pennsylvania, or California would be more attractive to the Democratic leaders than a man from Mississippi.

In the same way a Republican aspirant from Vermont would stir little excitement among his party leaders. They feel that Vermont is safe for the Republicans, just as Mississippi is safe for the Democrats. Why, then, waste the nomination on a Vermonter? They would rather boost the candidacy of someone from an uncertain state, in the hope that he might bring precious votes into the Republican camp. Like the Democratic leaders, the Republican chiefs expect at the least that a candidate will carry his own state. So they, too, incline toward a man who may produce a prized crop of votes for his party.

Which are the favored states for presidential timber? A count of the home states of presidential candidates from both major parties shows the following:

STATES OF RESIDENCE, DEMOCRATIC AND REPUBLICAN
CANDIDATES FOR PRESIDENT 1832-1960

New York	20
Ohio	9
Illinois	7
California	4
Nebraska	3
New Jersey	3
Pennsylvania	3

This geographic factor may seem unreasonable and discriminatory. But it's a fact of politics just the same. The American political system makes it harder for candidates from some states than from others. This does not mean that the door is closed forever to ambitious men from safe states. In any great human drama such as a presidential election, anything can happen. Something that which was called impossible yesterday may become reality tomorrow. Up to the present, however, candidates from safe states, both Democratic and Republican, have been handicapped in the presidential race.

This brings us to the well-known doctrine of "availability."

This means that a candidate who wants to attract the serious attention of party leaders, must have a combination of qualities that make him "available." A candidate is available, in the political sense, if he has certain features that party leaders and bosses like. He must be someone they feel they can put across, somebody with class—a winner. Otherwise they may withhold their support. Without the active help of party leaders from all over the country, his chances of getting elected would be slight. This is why would-be candidates nurture the friendship of party chiefs in every corner of the nation.

Nelson Rockefeller, who wanted the Republican nomination in 1960, personally tested the power of party leaders. Long before the Republican convention, he stumped up and down the country, looking for support. He came to the unhappy conclusion that Republican leaders everywhere were solid for Nixon. The magic of Rockefeller's name and his strong record as governor of New York didn't help. At Christmas, 1959, Rockefeller announced that the men who controlled the Republican party had already made up their minds about somebody else. Rockefeller said he was not prepared to engage in a massive struggle to win them to his side.

The qualities that make a man available vary somewhat from one generation to the next. But most of the ingredients that go into this formula remain fairly steady. What makes a man available?

For one thing, he must be a man. While the day may yet come when a woman will seriously contend for the Presidency, up to the present no woman has stood a chance. A few have tried anyway. In 1872 Victoria Woodhull ran for President on the Equal Rights ticket after being nominated by their convention. She went to the polls to vote for herself, but this was before the time of woman suffrage, and she was turned away. The same party put up Belva Ann Lockwood for President in 1884 and 1888. In recent years several minor parties have named women as their vice presidential candidates.

Popular prejudice is so strong on this subject that it is seldom even discussed. For the foreseeable future no woman could expect to receive the nomination of either major party. The reason is simple: the party leaders are sure the American people would never vote for a woman candidate. Therefore the party leaders would not permit a woman to get the nomination. For there is one rule that every political worker swears by: elections are for the purpose of winning. All other aims are secondary. Victory at the polls is the big thing. Victory means jobs for needy and deserving party workers. Victory means power for the party. Victory means prestige and strength for the party command. Victory also means an opportunity for party leaders to put their program into effect, to make good their promises to the people, and to consolidate and build for the next fight. Without victory a party is hobbled until the next election. A defeated political organization may have trouble holding its ranks together because it can offer its workers little except hope; jobs are a stronger cement.

Theodore Roosevelt once summed it up in unforgettable words. In 1912, four years after he had completed his own Presidency, Theodore Roosevelt was eager for another try at the White House. But President William Howard Taft, who was then in office, wanted to stay on the job. Taft, with his control of the Republican political organization, had the backing of party leaders. This dismayed Roosevelt who had to run on the Progressive ticket. He complained that the "regular" Republicans, who sided with Taft, had the "loaves and the fishes." By this he meant that they could reward party workers with jobs, favors, and other benefits. Roosevelt could appeal only to their spirit and to their personal loyalty.

Defeat at the polls causes party lines to sag. Party workers tend to lose interest; some drift away. Damage to the party organization may be considerable. Great energy is therefore spent to ensure victory. The greatest energy, of course, is expended in a presidential election, where the rewards for the victor are most abundant. A recent book on the Presidency says that both parties follow this principle: "win the election; never mind the expense; a defeat is the most expensive of all contests." It is easy to understand, then, why party leaders want a sure winner as their presidential candidate. It is clear also why they would not take the risk of bringing forward a woman candidate. To do so would be to ask for defeat.

To be politically attractive the candidate must usually have had substantial experience in public life. Such experience might well be as governor of a big state, or United States Senator, or Cabinet member, or Vice President, or as head of an embassy or of a big public international agency. Apparently it helps, too, if the man with presidential ambitions has been a lawyer. The history of both major parties shows that the private occupation of most candidates has been the law.

A man who has had experience as an important administrator in government stands a good chance. There are exceptions, of course. In 1940 Wendell Willkie, a lawyer and utility-company executive, surprised the politicians by capturing the Republican nomination. He lacked the political experience and the reputation that candidates usually bring to a nominating convention. But the unexpected can always happen at a big, sprawling convention. It may erupt into an open fight, it may be stampeded by the emotional appeal of an unknown or obscure figure. Willkie's 1940 nomination was a wild upset to tough, seasoned Republican leaders and bosses. But his hard, unsparing campaign did not bring Willkie the Presidency he cherished. He was overwhelmed at the polls by Franklin D. Roosevelt, an experienced public administrator.

A candidate's availability is helped if he is not too sharply identified with either labor or big business. A man whose career has been spent as leader of a labor union would not be available. Party leaders would regard him as too vulnerable. They would be thinking ahead to what the opposition would say of him—or throw at him—during a campaign.

A trade-union official, a labor leader, would be an easy target for abuse. He would be accused of being partial to labor and hostile to business and to our system of private ownership. He would be accused of plotting to establish a "laboristic" government that would favor the working class at the expense of all other Americans. He would be charged with wanting to squander government funds for housing, for rebuilding cities, for public low-cost medicine, for education, for helping the farmers, for expanding social security benefits. He would be attacked for wanting an extravagantly expensive program; one that would unbalance our budget, force taxes upward, and perhaps bankrupt the country. His opponents would claim that his plans would weaken our nation and expose it to easy assault by our enemies. They would try to dredge up evidence to show that somewhere, in his past, he had shown an interest in socialistic or communistic ideas. This could very well finish him off as a candidate and this is why a labor man would not be considered available for the presidential nomination by party leaders.

Just as a labor leader could not be a strong candidate, so would it be difficult for a big businessman to become available. In 1912 William Jennings Bryan steered the Democratic National Convention away from the "big business" candidate, Bennett Champ Clark, toward Woodrow Wilson. Bryan did this even though he had no affection for Wilson. Bryan was convinced that Clark was the spokesman for a group of selfish millionaires. The assembled Democratic chieftains believed Bryan and followed his signal to Wilson.

In 1840 the Whigs, ancestors of today's Republicans, nominated General William Henry Harrison for President and John Tyler for Vice President. The Whig politicians could have chosen a more prominent party leader—Henry

Clay. But in spite of Clay's services to the Whig party and to the country, he was bypassed in favor of a military hero whose war record could easily be inflated for publicity purposes. The politicians feared that Clay, a strong and outspoken leader in Congress, had made too many enemies, that he would be too vulnerable as a presidential candidate. In short, they decided he was not available.

Henry Clay's bitter disappointment is easy to understand. "My friends are not worth the powder and shot it would take to kill them. . . . I am the most unfortunate man in the history of parties: always run by my friends when sure to be defeated, and now betrayed for a nomination when I, or anyone, would be sure of election."

General Harrison, on the other hand, had not antagonized anybody. He was well remembered for his 1812 military victory at Tippecanoe and this made him a natural for presidential ballyhoo.

A Democratic writer had foolishly said of Harrison, "Give him a barrel of hard cider, settle a pension of two thousand dollars a year on him and . . . he will sit for the remainder of his days in his log cabin . . . studying moral philosophy." The fact is that General Harrison was a fairly wealthy man. But the Whig politicians seized their cue and created the image of a candidate who was earthy, simple, unsophisticated. They launched an eye-popping, ear-splitting, cider-guzzling campaign for "Tippecanoe and Tyler, too." They made the log cabin and the cider barrel familiar, welcome symbols. People liked the idea that candidate Harrison was a homespun type. They liked his war record. They also liked the cider that flowed freely at Harrison campaign rallies.

In 1940 Wendell Willkie captured the Republican nomination, even though he was the leader of a big utility corporation. In his campaign Willkie spoke plainly and looked a bit rumpled. Perhaps this was his way of overcoming his big-business background. But the enemy lost no chance to needle Willkie on the source of his wealth.

There have been other rich men who have been nominated in both parties. Some have partially overcome the handicap of wealth by fighting for policies that appealed to middle-class and working-class voters. In this group would be Theodore and Franklin Roosevelt and John F. Kennedy. Franklin Roosevelt was even called a traitor to his class. Aligned against him in the 1936 campaign was the "Liberty League" made up of prominent business leaders and millionaires. FDR twitted the Liberty League during the campaign. He convinced many voters that the League was not much interested in liberty for the poor man, the job-hungry worker and his family. Instead, said FDR, the Liberty League was really worried about the liberty of rich men to get richer.

Millionaire Nelson Rockefeller was a strong possibility for the 1960 Republican nomination, though his family's name for generations had been the symbol of arrogant, grasping wealth. But for years before the 1960 convention the Rockefeller family had been giving large sums of money to promote scientific, medical, and educational progress in the United States and abroad. Nelson Rockefeller had built a reputation as an earnest public servant in the administrations of Presidents Roosevelt, Truman, and Eisenhower. As governor of New York he had fought for laws that appealed to labor and working-class groups. He was, in other words, considered a liberal, social-minded Republican. His huge family fortune was no longer a political handicap.

Most rich candidates have had tough going in their campaigns. It's been easy to accuse them of favoritism to the business class, of prejudice against the working people, of indifference to the people's wish for better housing, better schools, low-cost medical care, and protection against the hazards of old age. A big-business candidate would surely be attacked by his opponents as an errand boy of Wall Street, as a tool of the bankers and the business class, as a man who is cold to the problems of ordinary people, and whose heart is shaped like a dollar sign. A rich businessman, in other words, is not a promising candidate, unless he has other qualities that offset his disadvantages.

Other characteristics that help decide availability are race and religion. In the foreseeable future only a white man stands a chance of winning the Democratic or Republican nomination. It may be that someday a Negro or a Chinese American may succeed in capturing the prize; but ingrained feelings on this subject are so strong that practically speaking, only a white candidate could be considered eligible.

Early in the Kennedy administration the President's younger brother, Attorney General Robert Kennedy, said, "There is no question about it. In the next forty years a Negro can achieve the same position that my brother has." This statement startled many, infuriated some, and seemed to others both unrealistic and unnecessarily provocative. Few experts could be heard to agree with the youthful Attorney General. Most thought that he was far off the beam.

Neither a Jew nor a Moslem has much of a chance, either. Until the 1960 election most of the books on presidential elections said that no Jew or Moslem or Catholic stood a chance. But starting in 1928, this solid political principle began to show cracks. That year, Roman Catholic candidate Al Smith was defeated in an election filled with religious bitterness. While many Americans voted against Smith because he was a Catholic, many other Americans—Protestants, Jews, and others—voted for him, even though he was a Catholic. Smith's name was placed in nomination at the 1928 Democratic National Convention by a prominent Protestant, Franklin D. Roosevelt. A great effort was made by Smith's friends of all faiths to put him into the White House. They failed in their aim. Many people took this to mean that a Catholic could never win the Presidency. But the nation had been exposed to the idea that a Catholic might run for the country's highest office. And millions of non-Catholics had actually voted for a Catholic. They had scaled the wall of prejudice.

The issue of religion was quiet for a long time after 1928. In the 1956 Democratic convention the vice presidential candidacy was thrown wide open by Adlai Stevenson, who had just been nominated as President. A Roman Catholic, John F. Kennedy, came surprisingly close to winning second place on the ticket, though he was finally beaten by Estes Kefauver.

Right after the 1956 convention, Kennedy began laying plans to win the Democratic presidential nomination in 1960. As he traveled everywhere in the country to line up votes for 1960, the question of his religion came more and more into the open. As the convention grew closer, and Kennedy began to look like a winner, the religion issue was debated more intensely. This continued through the convention period and became even more violent after Kennedy won the nomination. His candidacy drew support from some quarters and hot anger from others because of his religion. But on election day millions of Americans went to the polls to vote for Kennedy and demonstrate that they did not regard his religion as a bar to the highest office in the land.

The 1960 election was a landmark in establishing that a Catholic could win the Presidency. This does not mean that religion has been eliminated as a factor in deciding whether a man is available as a candidate. Political leaders still believe that at the very least a candidate must be a Christian and a churchgoer. To be available, a man must not be regarded either as an atheist or as opposed to religion. Any such views would almost surely eliminate him from consideration as a candidate.

There are other qualities, too, that are required of the successful candidate. These requirements would have puzzled Thomas Jefferson or Andrew Jackson or Abraham

Lincoln or Calvin Coolidge. It is nevertheless true that today's candidate must be a fairly skillful speaker on radio and he must perform passably well on television. Such phrases as "photogenic appearance" and "television personality" are now applied to presidential candidates. A man who speaks poorly on radio, whose physical appearance and manner do not register well on television, would be at a disadvantage in the battle for the nomination. So much campaigning is now conducted in these two media, that a candidate must be able to handle both.

The television debates between candidates Nixon and Kennedy in 1960 are widely regarded as the turning point in the campaign. Kennedy made the most of his opportunity to go before a huge audience. The candidates and their managers probably underestimated the drawing power of the debates. Somewhere between 110,000,000 and 120,000,000 people watched at least one of the debates. This seems to have set a record since the start of television.

While Nixon was better known to the country when the debates began, he lost his advantage as the contests continued. Kennedy, through his debating skill, dispelled the idea that he was inexperienced and immature. He appeared instead as a serious, informed student of national and international affairs; as a man who could think on his feet; as a youthful leader who could hold his own with worthy competition. He prepared thoroughly for his television appearances. With his close advisers he held lengthy "skull sessions" in which they briefed him on the subjects that were sure to come up during the debates. By the time he went before the cameras, Kennedy had the solid foundation of facts he needed to handle Nixon and the newspaper reporters who would ask questions.

Nixon, on the other hand, seems to have believed that Kennedy would show up as boyish, unprepared, deficient in background and experience. The Vice President did not, apparently, feel it necessary to put much time into preparation for the contest. He, and his supporters, were in for a shock.

Should Vice President Nixon have declined to debate with the Senator who was much less known? Some Nixon advisers thought so. Others had in mind this devastating possibility: Candidate Kennedy would go on television anyway and needle the absent Nixon, for whom an empty chair would be conspicuously provided.

A candidate's availability is helped if his personal life conforms to usual middle-class standards. Preferably he should not have been divorced, though Adlai Stevenson, a divorced man, carried the Democratic standard in both 1952 and 1956. The candidate should be what the American people like to call a "family man"—a devoted husband and father. A quality of steadiness and serenity endears a candidate to many voters. A bachelor, a man-about-town, a man with rotating lady friends would not be as available as a man who has settled down with his wife and, preferably, children. In some countries the private life of a candidate for high office is secure from public knowledge and discussion. In the United States, the candidate's personal affairs become subjects for probing and public debate.

While the Presidency obviously demands high intelligence, the American people have not been enthusiastic about placing an intellectual in the office. They want their President to be a leader, a man of action, a successful administrator, an experienced politician. But they do not seek scholars, thinkers, or philosophers for the Presidency. If a candidate has the primary qualifications and, at the same time, has superior intelligence, that does not disqualify him; but the American voters seems to distrust the highly intellectual candidate who lacks a down-to-earth, rugged quality. They know that the Presidency requires generalship, the ability to command, to inspire the loyalty of followers, to make decisions and stick with them. They rate these qualities as more important than a lofty I.Q.

In both 1952 and 1956 the Democrats put forward Adlai Stevenson, a man of great intelligence. His speeches had originality and rare humor. Seldom if ever in American history has a candidate spoken with such wit or freshness of style. Some of his speeches, in fact, were not fully understood by his listeners. How did the American people react? Mostly without enthusiasm. They preferred the plain syntax and the scrambled metaphors of Dwight Eisenhower. The voters were not ready to place their confidence in an intellectual; they seemed to feel more at home with the general who spoke uninspired prose. They believed that somehow an "egghead," as the Republicans labeled Stevenson, was not sufficiently practical to be entrusted with the Presidency.

In the 1960 campaign John F. Kennedy, author of two books, went before the American voters to ask their support. They saw in him a hard-driving, seasoned politician. They did not hold it against him that he was also bright. One British author summed up this strange feature of American presidential politics. The American people, he said, want their President to be "an uncommon man of common opinions." He should, in other words, be intelligent but not show it.

Adlai Stevenson expressed it another way. He had lost to Kennedy at the 1960 Democratic convention, but campaigned hard for his former rival. At a presidential rally in East Los Angeles the eloquent Stevenson introduced Candidate Kennedy and, in effect, told the difference between Kennedy and himself. In ancient Rome, said Stevenson, when Cicero had finished speaking the people said, "How well he spoke." But, added Stevenson, when Demosthenes had finished speaking the people said, "Let us march."

Summarizing, then, we have quite a list of unwritten requirements for the Presidency:

the right geography
the male sex

experience in public service
identification with neither big business nor labor
race
religion
skill as a radio and television personality
unblemished personal life
vigorous health
a politician's skill
intelligence
ambition
a feeling for people
a quality of moderation that gives him wide appeal

It is because of these rigorous qualifications that the experts say our nation of a hundred and eighty million people can yield only a hundred men who measure up. These requirements may change, of course, but at the present time a man who wants to be taken seriously by either party must have the right combination of the above qualities. This does not mean, of course, that every presidential candidate will have all these attributes. But this is the yardstick against which presidential aspirants are measured. The more abundantly a man is endowed with these characteristics, the hotter he becomes as a presidential possibility.

In addition to the openly available candidates, there are several other species of would-be Presidents. There is, for example, the "favorite son." He might be a state governor who has not won national enthusiasm for his candidacy. He might nevertheless control the convention delegates of his own state and this could be a sizeable asset. Such a favorite son has several possible courses of action. He may hold his delegates firmly in line at the convention and expect them to support his candidacy. Or he may use his strength for bargaining purposes. He might, for example, free them after one or two ballots, or he might swing them to another candidate at a strategic moment. To know when to hold tight, when to let go, and when to swing a delegation calls for political cunning and skill. If he times his action well, a favorite son can make a great deal of a relatively small thing. If he yields his delegates at the moment another candidate needs them to win, the favorite son may exact a high price for the votes he controls.

At the 1932 Chicago Democratic convention, Franklin D. Roosevelt was short of the required two-thirds of the delegates' votes. John Garner of Texas was persuaded to trade his slight presidential chances for a safe place on the ticket —as vice presidential candidate. Garner's support helped Franklin Roosevelt amass the two-thirds majority which at that time was still needed to win a Democratic nomination.

But Franklin Roosevelt probably wouldn't have made it without the help of the powerful newspaper publisher, William Randolph Hearst. In this strange political minuet, the omnipotent Hearst put pressure on the Texan and Californian leaders to go to Roosevelt. Hearst had no affection for Roosevelt, but he hated the other candidates who were considered strong—Newton Baker and Al Smith. So the Roosevelt-Garner ticket was created.

Sometimes a favorite son clings to the role too long. Many witnesses felt that New Jersey's Governor Meyner did this at the 1960 Democratic convention. Support for John F. Kennedy had been building up everywhere. Well in advance of the balloting, it looked like a Kennedy nomination. Governor Meyner was urged by many of his followers to forget about being New Jersey's favorite son and climb on the Kennedy bandwagon. Some of his supporters were themselves restless to get aboard with a sure winner before it was too late. The strategists of the Kennedy machine were pressing hard to entice or persuade or panic their opponents into joining up before the first balloting. This effort was having marked success—but not with Governor Meyner.

The New Jersey favorite son resisted all pressure, arguing that the convention should have the chance to select from a variety of nominees. Meyner's critics claimed that the governor, in going before the convention as a candidate, was selfishly insisting on having his moment of glory; that in letting himself be nominated he was hopelessly bucking the Kennedy tide; that the sensible thing for Meyner to do was to withdraw as a candidate and support Kennedy while it counted. In this way, the argument ran, New Jersey's Democrats and Governor Meyner himself would be assured of favorable consideration by Kennedy after the election.

In spite of strong feelings in the New Jersey delegation, Governor Meyner held to his course. He was duly nominated at the convention. The television audience saw a lively demonstration on his behalf, and he was recorded as a bona fide candidate for the Democratic nomination. The rest is familiar history: Kennedy's strength was so great that he buried all other candidates before the first ballot was ended. Wyoming gave him the votes he needed to win, and in the explosion that followed, Missouri's voice could be heard to nominate John F. Kennedy by acclamation. All other candidates, favorite sons included, went up in smoke.

Another variety of presidential candidate is produced in a "draft." Experts differ on the meaning of the word, and even on the question of whether there is such a thing. In theory, a draft means that the citizens decide on a desirable candidate and insist that he accept the job. This is in line with a belief that the office should seek the man, and not the other way round. There is much skepticism about this theory. Seasoned politicians seem to feel that no draft is bona fide; that to win the presidential office requires a complicated, expensive network of organization. It takes a willing, or eager, candidate to cooperate with the drafters. So while a particular candidate may appear to have been drafted, he has probably done a great deal of huffing and puffing to get the draft started.

Probably the bluntest words on this subject were spoken in 1960 by a man who knew American history and who had served a lifetime in politics—former President Harry Truman: "This draft business," he said, "is hooey. There never was a man drafted for President in the history of the country. A draft is created by the fellow who wants it and is willing to fight for it."

President Calvin Coolidge seemed to be inviting a draft in 1928 when he spoke the famous words: "I do not choose to run for the Presidency in 1928." People were puzzled by the declaration. Did Coolidge mean he didn't want another term? Did he mean he considered himself a two-termer already, because he had finished Harding's unexpired term and had been elected on his own in 1924? Did he mean that he relished another term but wanted to be drafted for it?

Lots of people thought back to General William Tecumseh Sherman's words when he was being pressured to run for President: "If nominated I will not accept; if elected I will not serve." The Sherman boom evaporated at this point. All presidential declinations since then have been measured against Sherman's words.

Franklin Roosevelt seemed to want a draft in 1944. World War II had almost been won and he was tired after twelve years in office. Up to convention time he said little about his candidacy. In the meantime his friends worked zealously to force a draft. Just before the start of the convention, Roosevelt signaled his lieutenants that he was ready and the fourth-term draft began blowing.

The New York Times believed that Adlai Stevenson's nomination in 1952 was the first genuine draft in American history. Certainly Stevenson did not actively seek the nomination. At most he was a reluctant candidate. In 1956 he was less reluctant, but in 1960 he again made it difficult for his followers to put him across. He gave no apparent cooperation in the 1960 campaign to the many groups who wanted him to get the nomination. Then, almost at the start of nominating, in recognition of the wildly emotional support that erupted all around him, Stevenson nodded Yes. In the meantime other candidates were fighting aggressively for the honor. From among them came the winner—John F. Kennedy.

Another reluctant candidate was Dwight Eisenhower, who required vigorous persuading before he agreed to run. The Democrats sought him as their standard bearer in 1948, without success. The Republicans worked hard to convince him to run under their banner in 1952. He finally yielded, though many people felt he did not want the office.

In addition to favorite sons, drafted candidates and reluctant ones, there is another species—the dark horse. This, supposedly, is the unknown candidate who bursts upon the convention at the right moment and becomes the happy choice of competing factions. Most dark horses have been less dark than is commonly supposed. William Jennings Bryan has usually been identified as a dark horse. He swung the 1896 Democratic convention on the strength of a single speech. Appealing to the convention to support the unlimited coinage of silver, he convinced the delegates that his formula was just what the plain people—farmers and factory workers— needed. He would give the country cheap, abundant money by drawing on the huge silver deposits that were being ignored in favor of gold.

Bryan satisfied the assembled politicians that America's working class would rally to the party if it adopted a Bryan platform. The big silver miners, relishing the prospect of a boom in their industry, were also eager to join up.

Said Bryan to the convention:

> We are fighting in the defense of our homes, our families, our posterity. . . . We have petitioned, and our petitions have been scorned. We have entreated, and our entreaties have been disregarded. We have begged, and they have mocked when our calamity came. We beg no longer, we entreat no more, we petition no more. We defy them! Having behind us the producing masses of this nation and the world . . . we will answer their demand for a gold standard

by saying to them: 'You shall not press down upon the brow of labor this crown of thorns! You shall not crucify mankind upon a cross of gold!'

Having hypnotized his audience, Bryan emerged as the unexpected choice of the convention and the leading figure in the Democratic party for the next twenty years.

One of the few people in the convention hall who was not surprised, apparently, was Bryan himself. It turned out that his "cross of gold" speech had been well tried out. Bryan knew that he had verbal magic in this oration and he used it for all it was worth. He expected a strong reaction from the convention and he got it.

Another dark horse was Warren G. Harding who in 1920 won the surprise nomination of the Republican party under conditions that will be described later. Because of his innocent, inoffensive record as a Senator, Harding had no enemies and lots of friends. Men who could not or would not support the leading candidates were willing to back a man of mediocre talents—a man whose record showed no great blunders and no achievements. But the qualities that made him the most available candidate in the 1920 Republican convention also made him unfit to be President.

It has been claimed by some writers of history that Harding's nomination and election in 1920 prove that able men do not become President under our system; that strong leaders—men who have made decisions and therefore made enemies—are eliminated and cannot win a nomination. But Harding's election doesn't prove this at all. It does establish that in special conditions a dark horse can be nominated and elected. It is an unhappy coincidence that Harding's performance in office was way below the average of American Presidents.

The political parties know it is to their advantage to elect strong rather than weak Presidents. A Chief Executive who is not qualified, who performs poorly, is a bad risk for any party. When the party nominates a man for the first time, they are thinking ahead, asking themselves whether their choice will wear well, whether he will still be serviceable four years later. They want a man who can run up a good record; a record they can display to the voters in the next election.

At the end of the first four-year term the party is obliged to renominate him. To do otherwise is to repudiate him and all he stands for.

Party leaders want a winner—not for one term but for two. They depend on him for their bread and butter, or as Theodore Roosevelt put it, for their "loaves and fishes." So their choice is a serious matter. Their own survival depends on it.

Another factor that influences availability is the public-opinion poll. There are a number of opinion-taking agencies in the country. Some, like Gallup and Roper, are well known. Others work mostly on a private, confidential basis. They all operate in roughly the same way. They sample the feelings of just a few thousand people. These people are selected from all over the country in careful proportions—so many farmers, so many housewives, so many lower, middle, and upper class citizens; so many factory workers or office workers or professional men. The pollsters try to get a cross section of the American people. They assume that the population as a whole will feel just about the same as the cross section they have questioned.

A candidate who shows strength in the pre-convention poll has a head start. He appears to the public—and that includes convention delegates—as a man who has already won a measure of public acceptance. He therefore commands serious attention. A candidate who shows up poorly in the advance poll-taking is at a disadvantage. He must win recognition in spite of negative omens.

This brings us to the primaries, which are discussed in detail in the next chapter. It need only be said here that in some states, primary elections are held in the months before the national nominating conventions. These primaries give the voters a chance to show how they feel about the men who want to be tapped by their party as presidential nominee. Sometimes the results of primaries carry weight at a convention, sometimes not.

The road to the presidential nomination is mined with high explosives. Nevertheless, every four years the Democratic and Republican conventions do produce a candidate apiece. One of them becomes President of the United States. This is the objective. This is the justification for the whole exciting, exhausting, expensive business.

Who stands a chance? A limited number of men in the whole nation. From among this small number emerge the active candidates. Some plan their campaign in amazing detail and go forward, step by step, on the path they think will take them to the White House. John Kennedy is a good example of this group. He began his drive for the 1960 Presidency as the 1956 Democratic convention folded its tents. Other men who aspire to the Presidency follow a different course. In the 1960 contest Senator Lyndon Johnson of Texas watched developments, hoped that other candidates would eliminate each other and that he would emerge as the all-around choice of the convention. So did Senator Stuart Symington of Missouri. Other aspirants, too, stood just outside the spotlight, ready to jump in at a moment's notice.

Nobody can guarantee which method will produce the cherished result. There are too many variables—too many people, too many pressures, too many chances for mishap— to be able to figure it out. But whatever style the winner uses, it has served the purpose—to give the United States a man who can handle the toughest job in the world.

CHAPTER THREE

THE CONVENTION

HALF CIRCUS AND HALF SUPREME COURT!

A ghastly travesty!

An undignified, disorderly, political rally!

An affront to American intelligence!

A sprawling mass meeting controlled by a small powerful clique!

These are some descriptions of the conventions held every four years by the major political parties to nominate a President of the United States. Even stronger language has been used by some observers to express their feelings about these quadrennial meetings.

Are these statements justified? Are the conventions merely an embarrassing relic of a bygone era? Is the delegates' behavior a true measure of the importance and the achievements of the national nominating conventions? If the conventions are as bad as people say, what can we do about it? What substitute can we find that will do the job better? Let's try to answer these questions.

First of all, we must remember that the national nominating convention was developed to fill a need—to nominate a party's candidate for President of the United States. Back in George Washington's day there was no such thing as a nominating convention because none was necessary. The men who wrote the Constitution never thought of it and made no provision for it. Their idea was simple. Electors—a small, select group of leaders in each state—would name the two outstanding men in the country. The man named by most electors would become President. The man who was second highest would become Vice President. The electors, men of property and wealth, could be relied on to make the right choice. In a country of small distances—remember we're talking about an eastern-seaboard nation of thirteen states— this was a good plan. Besides, the Founding Fathers had one candidate in mind when they wrote the Constitution, and that was George Washington. Everybody knew he would be the unanimous choice of the electors because he stood out in the nation in a way equaled by no other American since.

The Constitution-makers assumed that every four years a similar procedure could and would be followed. They did not foresee the rise of competing political parties with different interests and different principles. They did not envision the moving frontier that would eventually reach the Pacific— and then Alaska and Hawaii. The Founding Fathers could not have pictured the modern United States, with its varied geographic regions, its abundant agriculture, its numberless industries, its rich resources. Above all they could not fore- tell the growth of classes in the United States—the business class, the farming class, the laboring class, the managerial class, the white-collar class—each with a special way of look- ing at its own problems and the problems of the nation.

These are some developments the Founding Fathers could not possibly have known. They planned a government for a small agricultural society that grew into the most complex technological nation in the world.

It was inevitable, of course, that as the nation grew and as industries multiplied, these changes would affect politics. Politics, after all, is the machinery by which men try to obtain for themselves and their neighbors the best conditions for living and working.

The harmony that existed in 1789, when Washington was inaugurated, was shattered even before his first term expired. Already, two political camps had formed, one around Alexander Hamilton, the other around Thomas Jefferson.

These leaders had different ideas about governing the United States. Since their day, there has continued to be divided opinion about national policies—how our government should be run, and what responsibilities it should assume both at home and in the world. Sometimes there have been half a dozen or more national parties, each proclaiming its own answer to the nation's problems, and each demanding the right to govern the country.

This is a good place to stop and look at some of the smaller parties on the political landscape. In the 1960 election, for example, there were fourteen candidates, in addition to Democratic and Republican, vying for the Presidency. In some cases a candidate was supported by more than one party. The names of the sponsoring parties give some clue as to their leading principles. Here they are: Conservative Party of Virginia, Constitution Party, Tax Cut Party, Prohibition Party, Socialist Workers' Party, Farmer Labor Party of Iowa, Socialist Workers and Farmers Party of Utah, National States Rights Party, American Vegetarian Party, Socialist Labor Party, Industrial Government Party, Afro-American Unity Party, American Third Party, Conservative Party of New Jersey, Greenback Party, American Beat Consensus, Constitution Party of Texas.

Each of these minor parties, sometimes called "third parties" or "splinter parties," has a central purpose. Each believes that it has the answer to the nation's main problems and, once it gains power, can put the nation on the right track.

Do these third parties really believe they can win? Some do. Certainly they work at it with much heart. But the results have seldom been impressive. There are exceptions, though. In the election of 1924 Robert LaFollette, candidate of the Progressive party, amassed almost five million votes. This was an all-time high for a third party. Usually the results are sad.

Why, if the third parties are doomed to fail, do they continue to compete with the big, rich, and powerful Democratic and Republican parties? Because they are fighting for a principle. They want to get their story before the American people, to get the widest public attention for their point of view. There is always a chance of picking up new recruits. Then, in addition, they continue to hope that lightning might strike, that they might actually come up with a winner.

No third party has ever won a national election or even come close. The American people have generally said "Ho hum" as third-party orators clamor for the chance to save the country.

Does this mean that third-party efforts are a huge waste of energy? Not necessarily. Some ideas that began in the platforms of third parties have later been adopted by the major parties. Third parties have again and again complained that the major parties have pirated their principles. Many of the humanitarian and social policies that today are accepted practice in the United States, were once the property of third parties. These include:

> the eight-hour day
> protection for women and children in industry
> workmen's compensation
> unemployment insurance
> old-age pensions
> government-supported education
> government-sponsored housing
> tenement-house and factory inspection

These examples show that third parties are a source of ideas for government. But aside from this, third parties constantly goad the two major parties to improve their performance. The third parties expose weaknesses in the Democratic and Republican parties and inspire them, or shame them, into doing better.

Third parties are living proof of political freedom. Any American who is dissatisfied with the major parties may turn to a third party. Or, if he can rouse others to agree with him, he may start his own third party and take it into the market place of ideas. He can put his own propaganda into competition with all the rest.

The right of dissent, of disagreeing with the majority and saying so out loud, is basic in a democracy. It is a good test of the vitality of free speech, free press, and free assembly. This means it is a good test of democracy itself.

While the American people have never voted for third parties in large numbers, they support the right of third parties to organize and to scour the nation for votes. This has been true almost from our beginning as a nation. There is no sign of any change today.

As the United States grew out of its infancy, it was clear, of course, that the system for nominating and electing a President would be changed. After George Washington, there was no longer a single leader who could command the affection and support of all the electors in all the states. This was proved again and again between the time of Washington and the 1830's, when the national nominating convention was born. Presidential candidates during most of this period were proposed by congressmen in secret party meetings called "caucuses." Such private meetings by party members are as old as politics itself, and continue, of course, right up to the present day. The electors in each state, it was hoped, would support the names that came out of the congressional caucus. For a time the state legislatures went into the business of nominating presidential candidates. Even the county courts in various states made nominations for President.

But these methods of proposing presidential candidates— in congressional caucus, in state legislatures, or by county courts in the states—were unsatisfactory. There was no way of controlling the number of candidates who might be nominated. The electors in the various states might be faced with a bewildering list of names—some familiar, some unknown—from whom a choice had to be made. Some better way of picking the party's national leader had to be worked out. So it was that the national nominating convention was invented.

The first national party convention was called in 1830 by the Anti-Mason party in Philadelphia. This group wanted most of all to prevent Andrew Jackson from winning a second term in 1832. It failed in its aim, of course, but it gave the two major parties an idea—they might hold a national party convention to nominate candidates for President and Vice President. Both the national Republican party and the Democratic party held nominating conventions within the next two years. The Democratic convention of May, 1832, meeting in Baltimore, endorsed Andrew Jackson for President. He had already been nominated by different groups around the country. This convention also approved Jackson's personal choice for Vice President, Martin Van Buren.

At this 1832 Democratic convention, incidentally, the famous "two-thirds rule" was passed. This required that a candidate, to win the nomination, had to obtain the votes of two-thirds of the convention delegates. It obviously meant, also, that one-third of the delegates plus one, could withhold the prize from any Democrat. This gave any minority group in the Democratic party considerable power.

This two-thirds rule stirred bitter objections. Many party leaders felt it was undemocratic, that it placed excessive power in the hands of a minority. But it remained in effect in the Democratic convention until 1936, when Franklin Roosevelt won his four-year battle to change it. The Democratic party then adopted the majority rule that the Republicans had always followed.

Just what happens at a present-day national nominating

convention? Delegates from every state and territory come together after a four-year interval to name their presidential standard bearer. Originally there were to have been as many delegates at each party convention as there were members in the combined houses of Congress. At the Democratic convention, for example, the state of New York would have one delegate for each of its members in the House of Representatives, plus two additional, to correspond to its Senators. In the Republican convention the same basis would be used. But this intended plan was abandoned by both major parties many years ago.

Why? Because pressure built up in each party to enlarge the number of delegates who might take part in choosing a presidential candidate. So a system of alternates was devised. Supposedly, for each voting delegate there should be an alternate to take over in the absence of the delegate. By this measure, the number of convention participants was doubled. The group was further increased by a system of "bonus" votes given to the states which had made a good record for the party in previous elections.

As the number of delegates in the Democratic party convention grew larger, somebody suggested giving each delegate a half vote. Every member of the group still voted, but his vote counted only for half. The Republicans have stuck with the policy of one delegate, one vote.

The crowd at the convention is expanded also by the presence of many convention officials who are not necessarily delegates. Also present is the national committee of each party, which has charge of all party affairs between elections. This is a powerful group of party people who deserve and expect to be recognized at the convention. Then there are many distinguished guests who must be invited. These may include high-ranking persons, in or out of office, who have served their party. And there are hundreds of leaders of organizations who want the convention to listen to their ideas. Many of these people are too important to be ignored.

There is also a huge assortment of official visitors and guests, some from the host city and others from the rest of the nation.

At the 1960 Democratic convention, a total of 1521 whole votes were cast; 761 were needed to nominate a candidate. At the Republican convention 1331 votes were cast; a majority was therefore 666 votes.

Yet the Democratic convention of that year attracted over 30,000 people. The proceedings at Los Angeles were brought to the world by more than five thousand members of the press, radio, and television corps. At the 1960 Republican convention in Chicago much the same happened. Though it started out to be a meeting limited to official delegates, each having one vote, the convention had become swollen to almost unmanageable size.

Where and when the convention meets is decided by the permanent committee of the party, whose headquarters are in Washington. Long before convention time, the national committees, both Democratic and Republican, receive bids from cities that would like to be host to the conventions. Businessmen in these cities are eager to attract the conventions because delegates spend money on hotels, food, entertainment, souvenirs, sight-seeing. Usually, interested businessmen in a city contribute to a fund amounting to a few hundred thousand dollars which they offer to the national committee in return for the privilege of entertaining the convention.

The size of the financial offer made by the cities is important. National conventions and presidential campaigns are costly. The national committee, which is usually in debt, wants the biggest possible financial lift. Los Angeles offered the Democrats $450,000 in return for the right to play host to the 1960 convention.

The national committee considers many factors when making its choice. It wants to be sure that the city has adequate facilities—a big convention hall, ample hotel space, good transportation facilities. The local political picture can also affect the decision, especially if the area has a leading presidential candidate. Rival groups on the committee may work for or against a particular location, depending on the possible effects on their candidate's chances. Generally, a neutral ground will be favored, so that no candidate may win special benefit from having the convention in home territory.

After weighing all the issues, the national committee decides on a convention site. In 1960 the Democrats picked Los Angeles, the Republicans Chicago. Other favorite convention cities have been San Francisco, Philadelphia, Baltimore, Houston, St. Louis, and New York.

Weeks before the delegates gather, the convention city becomes an exciting, throbbing mecca. As the national political fever rises, all eyes turn on the scene of the convention. Party workers and the advance men of candidates, as well as representatives of press, radio, and television descend on the place. The presidential contenders have long since reserved choice hotel suites and working space in office buildings. Each, naturally, has sought the best possible locations for his activities. Campaign managers and their staffs show up early to do all possible missionary work before the convention opens. There are delegates and local citizens to be worked on and inspired and brought to fighting pitch, if possible. The managers and staff workers do everything they can to make the convention city itself solid for their candidate.

Arrangements are made for an army of press, radio, and TV people. This gets more complicated and more expensive all the time. Each of the 1960 conventions was outfitted with electronic equipment worth about $1,000,000.

Before the Democratic convention of 1960 opened in Los Angeles, the political organization of John Kennedy had planned in minute detail for its candidate. Governor Abraham Ribicoff, Kennedy's convention floor manager, had provided for the installation of sixty telephones to check developments on the convention floor. Before the sessions began, the Governor and young Robert Kennedy stationed the Kennedy workers at strategic points in the hall and drilled them in their duties. Their aim was to keep watch over all Kennedy delegates in the huge auditorium, to win new delegates when possible, and to dispatch instant help wherever trouble might develop. The Kennedy leaders wanted to be sure their candidate lost no supporters, that he gained new adherents, and that he moved steadily in only one direction—to the nomination.

Candidate Lyndon Johnson, when he found himself with only two floor telephones, complained loudly. His own workers had not planned their floor strategy with the thorough, meticulous care of the Kennedy group. Johnson, together with many other experienced politicians, was astounded more than once by the cold, pitiless efficiency of the Kennedy machine.

As delegates begin to arrive in the convention city, they are usually greeted by groups of lovely young ladies—many of them professional show girls—who are there to sing the praises of particular candidates. Such eye-filling beauties are pretty much required for a leading contender. Some candidates, who are unwilling or unable to bear the cost, dispense with this esthetic touch. A few candidates, who are themselves very popular, may have volunteers—in all shapes and sizes—who will advertise their candidacy without pay.

The official delegates are quickly caught up in the carnival spirit of the convention city. Every form of advertising and ballyhoo is used by the various campaign managers to haul delegates into camp. Telegrams and personal letters of welcome from the different campaign headquarters await many delegates as they check in at their hotel rooms. Delegates are invited to meet the candidates and to be their guests at receptions that may provide anything from punch and cookies to sumptuous dining. Leaders of delegations, usually governors or big city and state bosses, are pursued with special energy. The candidates and their top managers usually concentrate on these key delegates. Various lures are used—hints or promises of jobs, an open door at the White House when final victory has been won, the assurance that the President-to-be will listen attentively to future requests.

All candidates maintain headquarters as near as they can get to the convention hall. Here, depending on the financial resources of the candidate, the hungry or thirsty delegate, and his wife and family and friends, can find a cheerful welcome and some sort of refreshment.

Before the official opening of the convention, many delegations meet in caucus. At these closed meetings, the delegates decide how they will vote on candidates and on platform issues. These caucuses are supposed to be private, but their proceedings usually leak out, especially if there is divided opinion on how the delegates should vote. Some caucuses invite the leading presidential hopefuls to visit and answer delegates' questions. Such a caucus may offer a contender a chance to make a strong pitch to a group of delegates. At such a meeting he may make friends who will come through for him later, when the balloting takes place. Some of them, who may not feel free to vote for him on the first ballot, might decide to support him on the second, third, or fourth.

The rules by which convention delegates are elected vary from state to state. Some delegations are the disciplined followers of a powerful state or city leader. He may have put their names on the county, district, or state lists that are voted on by party members.

State conventions are held in about two-thirds of the states to elect delegates to the national party convention. These state meetings may also instruct the delegates for whom to vote at the national convention. Delegates from many of these states look to the party boss to call the signals. He decides when to switch his strength from one candidate to another; his block of votes can usually be counted on to stick together.

Some delegations are pledged to support a favorite son— a governor or senator, usually—for perhaps one ballot. After this complimentary vote, such delegates are either set free to vote their choice, or they may be required to stay in line behind their state boss.

In about one-third of the states the delegates are governed, more or less, by state presidential primary rules. The election laws in these states give the citizens of each party a chance to name their choice for President. In certain states the results of such elections are binding. The delegates from these states are fully committed by law. They must vote for the persons named by the citizens. These delegates are not subject to raids—not on the first ballot, anyway. Some states which conduct primary elections do not compel delegates to support the primary winner. The primary in such states is advisory rather than binding.

Presidential hopefuls think hard before entering a state primary. They prefer, of course, to enter "easy" contests. An example would be a state that had no powerful local rivals. But if a state has its own favorite son whose eye is on the White House, an outside candidate might hesitate to come in. No aspiring candidate wants to rouse the anger of a favorite son by raiding territory that is already staked out. There's another reason, too. It frequently happens that after the first or second ballot the favorite son melts away. Once he has gotten his limited number of complimentary votes, he might no longer be a serious competitor, but he might still be able to transfer his good will and his block of votes to some other hopeful. This is quite a prize. Therefore, few contenders care to antagonize a favorite son.

Another thing that deters candidates from entering state presidential primaries is the damage that results from losing such a contest. Press, radio, and TV make a big propaganda show out of every presidential primary election. These battles take place in the months before convention time when interest in presidential politics is mounting. A candidate who loses in one of these races may be finished as an aspirant for the Presidency. The odor of failure may attach itself to the loser and bar him from further consideration by the political leaders whose support is necessary in a campaign.

Defeat in a state primary might be the result of special conditions that should not influence a candidate's chances. Yet it has been shown several times—by candidate Willkie in Wisconsin's 1944 primary and by Harold Stassen in the 1948 Oregon primary—that a single primary defeat can eliminate a strong candidate from the whole presidential race. In neither case did these primaries show how the nation's Republicans felt about these candidates, but they were through just the same.

Just as a single primary failure can ruin a man's candidacy, so a series of successes can give him a hefty boost toward the party nomination. John F. Kennedy entered seven state presidential primary contests and won them all. At least four of these primaries were fairly safe. Two, Wisconsin and West Virginia, were tough. Defeat in any of them might have killed his candidacy. He took the risk because he wanted to demonstrate to the professional politicians and to the country that his youth and his Catholic faith would not bar his presidential candidacy.

When Kennedy won the primary in West Virginia, a strongly Protestant state, his presidential stock shot upward. He had made his point. He looked like a winner now. The concentration of national interest in this primary election meant that Kennedy could no longer be brushed off as an ambitious aspirant handicapped by his religion and his young appearance. He had made himself a front-runner.

The presidential primary was originally thought to be a great democratic improvement. The people in the states, it was hoped, would decide who the presidential candidates should be. This, presumably, would take the power of choice away from the professional politicians and place it where it belonged, with the people themselves.

It has not worked out this way. Most states never adopted the presidential primary. Where it has been enacted, the rules vary widely. Some states consider the results binding, some don't. The primaries are given so much publicity that their importance is inflated beyond reason. A single victory or a single loss may make or break a candidate. This is unfair.

Some people who have specialized in the study of presidential politics advise that the problem could be eased if all states adopted uniform primary rules and held these elections at the same time. Then, all over America on a given day, party members would name their choice for President. Later the Democratic and Republican conventions would ratify these choices and the campaign between the two rivals would begin.

There would obviously be advantages in such a plan. But there would be disadvantages, too. This policy would force the prospective candidates to campaign in all fifty states and the District of Columbia before the primary election took place. The winner of the primaries would then have to be endorsed by the party convention. After this he would have to campaign all over again against his rival from the opposing party. It is doubtful whether a candidate could stand the physical punishment or the expense of all this activity. It would probably drive away many good potential candidates.

Other experts think that the nationwide presidential primary simply could not do the job as well as the present-day nominating convention, where the decision is made by a few thousand delegates. Here, it is pointed out, the factions in each party can try to work out their differences. The result, usually, is that they name a presidential ticket they can live with. But could fifty separate state primaries achieve any such result? This group says No.

Still other authorities claim that the primary, however hopeful it may once have seemed, has been made obsolete by the public-opinion poll. According to this view, the feeling of party members is shown quickly, efficiently, and inexpensively by the polls. Presidential primaries, they argue, are now unnecessary. A few samplers of public opinion can tell within a few days just how much support the aspiring candidates have among the people in each party, they say.

Success in the 1960 presidential primaries of seven states shot John F. Kennedy into the first rank of Democratic aspirants. He believed that the presidential primary was a fair device for screening would-be candidates. It exposed the participants to public view and gave them a chance to test their strength in the national arena. Kennedy felt that the winners in the primaries must be taken seriously by the delegates gathered in the national party convention. Many people agree that even a few primaries are better than no primaries. They insist that this procedure places much of the power of decision with the people instead of leaving it all to political leaders at the convention.

Lyndon Johnson, on the other hand, felt that the business of the nominating convention was to "consult together" about possible candidates and to name the man who was best qualified by ability and experience for the awesome job of President. Convention delegates, according to Johnson, have a huge responsibility. In their deliberations they should not be influenced by the results of a few primary contests. Victories or defeats in individual state primaries might have little to do with the basic question—What member of the party is best equipped to lead the march to victory in the presidential election? In Johnson's view, primaries are local popularity contests, unrelated to the business of naming the party's best candidate.

To charge off in all directions, battling in one state primary after another is ridiculous, Johnson felt. The contender, realizing that a single defeat might be fatal to his prospects, is subjected to unnecessary strain. The whole thing, said Johnson, is pointless.

The differing points of view have their supporters. At one extreme are those who advocate an extension of the primary system to all the states. Others feel that primaries are useless or misleading and should be abolished altogether. In this latter group is former President Truman who publicly declared in the spring of 1960, "I hope that people have had a bellyful of these primaries. They are outrageously expensive and exhausting."

In their pursuit of the nomination, some men go before the convention as acknowledged, declared contenders. John F. Kennedy, from the time in 1956 when he lost the Democratic vice presidential nomination, became a 1960 presidential contestant. Though he didn't actually commit himself publicly until early in 1960, he had been traveling around the country for three years making the sounds of a determined competitor in the 1960 race.

The signs of delegate-hunting are well known. The aspirant shakes hands in counties all over the nation. If he can't find grownups, he greets children. He will try most anything that will get his name and his face before the community. He meets party leaders everywhere. He tries to develop a nucleus of friends and an embryo political organization in every district where this is possible. Eventually experts from his national headquarters arrive to give advice, leadership, and funds. They help to organize local clubs and stimulate the flowering of groups of dedicated followers.

Mr. Kennedy got substantial help from his clubs in each of the 1960 primaries he entered. Many of those who enrolled were willing to do the hard work of spreading the gospel and getting out the vote. They rang doorbells, conducted Kennedy socials, telephoned friends and neighbors, and ad-

dressed, sealed, and stamped mountains of Kennedy literature. These eager volunteers were fortresses of Kennedy
strength in hundreds of communities. An important feature
of the Kennedy clubs was their full-time staffs. Some of these
were paid workers. Others were sufficiently well-to-do to
take leaves of absence from their regular work to labor without pay for John F. Kennedy. Many of his competitors' clubs,
on the other hand, were open only on week ends because the
staffers had to earn a living. This made a difference.

Carefully, thoroughly, systematically, the Kennedy workers built a national network of clubs. These were tightly
organized and single-minded in their purpose—to put John
F. Kennedy into the White House. By July, 1960, nobody
doubted that Kennedy stood at the threshold of victory.

Other candidates play it differently. They remain "undeclared" though their actions betray that they are hard-
running contenders. Republican Thomas E. Dewey in 1944
maintained up to the moment of his nomination that he was
not a candidate.

Lyndon Johnson in 1960 was an undeclared contestant.
Like many another hopeful, he wanted the convention itself
to call him forward and place the coveted wreath on his
brow. He did a limited amount of presidential politicking,
while friends ran an unofficial, low-speed campaign designed
to keep his name at voters' eye level. He later explained that
he felt his first responsibility was to stay in Washington and
carry on as Senate majority leader. He could not, he said,
build a national organization to promote his presidential
ambition and at the same time do his duty as a lawmaker.
So he chose to do the latter. In saying this, Johnson took a
whack at young Senator Kennedy, who ran up an imposing
record of absence from his senatorial duties. Kennedy, of
course, had other serious business—to line up delegates to
the 1960 convention.

Johnson announced his candidacy only ten days before the
Democratic convention opened. By this time, the available

delegates had been pretty much corralled by his hard-working young rival, John F. Kennedy. On the first ballot the presidential hopes of all the undeclared and recently-declared aspirants went crashing. Mr. Kennedy proved that long, hard planning and politicking brought results.

Who are the approximately three thousand delegates who occupy the convention hall every four years? Newspaper and TV pictures of these meetings give an unflattering impression of the delegates. They may be shown as undisciplined, if not completely out of control, a holidaying group of aging adolescents. At the convention they may appear inattentive or openly bored. Their faces are sometimes buried behind newspapers. Frequently they are seen chatting among themselves while the chairman makes futile efforts to conduct an orderly meeting. Favorite TV shots show delegates munching hot dogs or sipping pop or yawning or enjoying horseplay while a high-powered orator is trying vainly to be heard.

Does this picture of a disorderly convention correspond to the facts? To a limited extent, yes. For one thing, the convention proceedings are drawn out to a week, though they could well be shortened. This fact alone helps explain why the delegates may appear relaxed—perhaps too relaxed. But the two national committees want to display the crucial portions of their show on television at hours when they can attract the biggest audience from all over the nation. To present just one main feature a day during prime television hours, they must stretch out the program. Also, the committees want to keep the delegates in town long enough for them to do their official duty, to have some fun, and to reward the businessmen who have given a big cash gift to the national party. Time must also be allowed for a lot of talking, and caucusing, and trading.

Remember, also, that much serious convention business takes place behind the scenes. For at least a week before the convention is called to order, the platform committee has been conducting hearings, studying different points of view and shaping the party platform. By the time the convention starts, the platform committee has pretty well completed its work. Similarly, the credentials committee has been judging the claims of competing delegations. This committee tries to decide which of two or more contesting groups truly represents the party of a certain state. This may be hard work. Both parties from time to time have had to choose between hostile rivals, each demanding to be recognized. The committee may be faced with a Solomon's choice of admitting one group and excluding their opponents.

Much of the oratory heard at the convention is "filler." It is hallowed by tradition and is expected by the delegates, even though they don't listen to it. While the speechmakers fill the air, a lot of negotiation between candidates and delegates takes place—on the convention floor and in side rooms, in candidates' headquarters, and in hotel rooms.

Generally the Democratic convention is considered less well-mannered than the Republican. Some observers have given reasons for this. Democrats, supposedly, are more emotional, more extroverted, more noisy and expressive. They have more disputes among themselves. They are more interested in the underdog—the poor, the underpaid, the aged, the underprivileged. The range of opinion among Democrats on any subject may be very wide. To bring the extremes together is hard and sometimes bloody.

The Republican delegates are said to be more sedate and dignified; they are more reserved in manner and behavior. They are likely to be wealthier and to worry more about protecting their investments and their property. They generally oppose having the federal government start big new projects in housing, medicine, education, and social security. Such activities mean a bigger, more powerful federal government. They also mean higher taxes. Delegates at the Republican convention are conscious of the impression they make before the country on TV, radio, and in the press, and they try hard to make it a good one.

Certainly a lot shows up on TV that is embarrassing. But the pattern of the national nominating conventions was set long before the days of TV. Exposure on millions of TV screens is a cruel new problem. It is hard for any large meeting to look good on TV. And the national nominating convention, in its nature, is badly adapted for TV showing.

Large groups of people, whether at a convention or a ball game, in a courtroom or theatre, on a busy crossing or at a parade, may look a bit laughable when caught by the TV camera. They yawn, they smirk, they giggle, they grab for attention. They sneeze and cough, look happy or woebegone, or completely preoccupied. This is what the convention TV picture may show, but is it a basis for condemning the convention?

Perhaps the important question is not, How does the convention look on TV? but rather, Does the convention do its job reasonably well? If so, then it's not too important whether the convention registers well on the nation's TV screens. Let's get a close-up of the delegates at work.

★　　　　　★

CHAPTER FOUR

"I GIVE YOU
THE MAN WHO..."

WHAT SORT OF PEOPLE COME TO THE NOMINATING CONVEN-
tion to pick "the man who" may lead the nation for the next
four or eight years? Generally the delegates are upper-mid-
dle-class Americans. They are people of financial substance
who hold fairly important positions in their own communities. They are big names in their political party, or they
would not have been tagged as convention delegates. Many
are active politically. Others are known chiefly as contributors of money, angels who keep the party afloat financially. To all of them, the delegate's badge is a symbol of
status in their home town. It is a recognized mark of prestige.
It identifies the wearer as one of a handful of people in the
nation who may help choose the next President.

Among the delegates are many public officials—county,
state, and national legislators; mayors, judges, governors,
senators. Some are names out of the past that are still
remembered. Some are venerated national leaders who
dignify the convention by their mere presence—former Presidents and the wives of former Presidents.

Sometimes a generous party member will assume the expense of a group of convention delegates. Usually, however, each delegate pays his own way. The cost—without including wife and family who might accompany him—is likely to be around a thousand dollars.

It is clear that however they may conduct themselves at the convention, the delegates are not a cross section of Americans. They are, instead, above average in wealth, in education, in social standing, in the positions of trust they hold. When we criticize them, let's remember we're talking about lawyers, businessmen, mayors, labor leaders, judges, important party workers, state legislators, congressmen, and senators—people who have achieved success in their chosen way of life. For these are the people who have the votes at the Democratic and Republican conventions.

Once the convention is called to order, the first important piece of business is the keynote speech. For this honor a prominent party member is selected. His purpose is to set the tone for the convention, to explain to the delegates and to the nation why his party must win the election. He is expected to warn the country of dire results if the other party should prevail. The keynoter is supposed to charge his listeners with revival-meeting fervor, to inspire them to rise above mere party politics and name a candidate who will bring victory to the party and glory to the nation.

Few keynote speakers disappoint their hearers. They always magnify their party's achievements. They always invoke the names of sainted party leaders who have made strong records. The Republicans take a backward, prideful look at Washington, Lincoln, Teddy Roosevelt, Eisenhower. The Democrats glow in the memory of Jefferson, Jackson, Wilson, and Franklin Roosevelt.

Many listeners are indifferent to the keynoter's claims. They do not believe that his party is as great as he says. Nor do they believe that the opposition is as villainous and corrupt as he charges. The more sophisticated listeners may even be amused by the keynoter's oratorical flights and obvious exaggerations. But the keynote address remains a durable fixture of the national conventions. There is no sign that either party is prepared to dispense with the combination of fact and hokum and self-glorification that makes up this ritual.

The delegates at both conventions go through certain mechanics of organization, though these are usually arranged in advance. These include the election of a permanent convention chairman. This officer wields much power. He has the authority to recognize a floor delegate, or to ignore him. When balloting takes place, his recognition may make or break a candidate's chances of winning the nomination. The chairman decides whether the Ayes or the No's have it, though everybody may disagree with him. At certain points in the balloting, there may be intense competition among the delegates for the honor of giving a particular candidate the votes that will put him over the top. By his nod the chairman may decide who shall taste a moment of fame. He can lift a group of delegates to the winner's bandwagon. With this same power he may determine who gets banished to outer darkness.

The acceptance of the platform is sometimes a routine matter, sometimes not. For days before the convention is called to order, committees and sub-committees listen to individuals and groups who plead for inclusion of their own ideas in the platform. Representatives of labor, business, farmers, minority groups of all kinds, and a host of others, will ask that the platform support their cause. Theodore White, an expert on presidential elections, calls these hearings an empty ritual, and says that the platform committees decide what gets written into the final statement. He also argues that the platform itself means little, that writing the document gives some political leaders a chance to be temporarily important. The man who wins the election, says White, decides how much of the platform—if any of it—is to be taken seriously.

Strenuous efforts are made by the platform committee to compose all differences before they give their statement to the public. Some platforms have been written and rewritten in a setting of violent disagreement. An example is the Republican platform of 1960. The liberal Republican wing, led by Governor Nelson Rockefeller, clashed with the conservatives. Candidate Nixon, eager for the friendship of the Rockefeller group, threw his weight behind their cause and a Rockefeller-style platform was put together.

In recent Democratic conventions the civil rights issue has burst open on the convention floor, where it became a subject of bitter debate before being put to a vote. This question has several times threatened to rupture the Democratic party.

Once the platform has been accepted, the next order of business is the nomination of candidates. For this purpose, an alphabetical roll call is held. As the clerk calls out the name of each state in turn, the chairman of each delegation may nominate a candidate, he may pass, or he may yield to another state. This is generally arranged in advance. A candidate may want a particular delegate, perhaps a homestater, to present his name to the convention.

The nominating speech is likely to fit a familiar pattern. It may last about fifteen minutes, though frequently more. The speaker, standing at the rostrum and looking out over thousands of delegates and gallery visitors, reads his speech from several teleprompters that face him on the platform.

At the 1960 Democratic convention in Los Angeles, the speaker stood on an elevator platform. This adjustable device made it possible for every speaker to stand at a uniform height as he read his comments to the audience. At one point the electrically operated platform moved in the wrong direction and Chairman Le Roy Collins suddenly found himself

towering above lectern and audience. He was finally lowered
to the proper height.

Nominating speeches generally follow a time-worn pattern. The orator punches away at one target: if ever the
nation was blessed with the right man, that time is now, and
his candidate is that man. The speaker works his way through
a long catalogue of virtues possessed by his nominee, who
is invested with qualities of greatness, if not immortality.

Each nominating speaker warms to his climax and then
caps his oration by giving the convention "the man who" will
save the country, if only he can have the chance. As the
speaker pronounces the magic name he triggers what is
called a spontaneous demonstration.

Much labor is spent in trying to make the outburst look
natural, self-igniting, and contagious. Rarely is it any of
these things. There are some outstanding exceptions, of
course. William Jennings Bryan set the 1896 Democratic
convention on fire with his "cross of gold" speech. The famous
"Willkie blitz" at the 1940 Republican gathering is another
example of a bona fide, unrehearsed show of feeling that
brought an unexpected nomination.

Observers agree that at the 1960 Democratic convention,
only one demonstration—for Adlai Stevenson—was wildly
emotional, uncontrolled, and genuine. It lasted eighteen pas-
sionate minutes, it was a prairie fire. But as old politician Jim
Farley noted, this demonstration was limited to friends and
admirers of Stevenson. The delegates sat on their hands.
With or without enthusiasm, they were planning to vote for
John F. Kennedy and they were not going to be led astray
by the emotional jag of a few hundred screaming, parading
partisans of Adlai Stevenson. Said Jim Farley, in summary,
"They don't win or lose a vote with the parading because
most of those who parade don't have the votes." Nevertheless,
some historians claim that Abraham Lincoln himself won the
Republican nomination in Chicago in 1860 because of an
organized claque. Under the sign, "Vox Populi, Vox Dei,"

they raised such a commotion for Lincoln that he won over a more prominent Republican, William H. Seward. Lincoln's managers, using forged admission cards, had seated a thousand supporters in places that belonged to Seward men.

But win or lose, the convention thunder rolls on. As the candidate's name is trumpeted forth, the commotion begins. Men and women come plowing into the aisles carrying the banners and standards and papier-mâché heads of their idol as they shriek his name. They snake dance through the hall trying to impress other delegates into their ranks or at least trying to convince them that this candidate has been tapped by destiny. The parading is often joined to horseplay as demonstrators and seated delegates try to make off with each other's banners and standards.

Sometimes the excitement is sustained only by the supreme efforts of loyal supporters. In the 1952 Republican convention, Senator George Bender of Ohio stood on the platform bellowing "Onward Christian Soldiers" again and again. He was determined to keep Robert Taft's demonstration going strong, no matter what the cost.

One of the weirdest efforts of this kind was expended on behalf of Franklin Roosevelt's third-term candidacy at Chicago in 1940. From under the convention platform, the Chicago Superintendent of Sewers brayed for Roosevelt in a voice that seemed to come from deep in the inner earth. In the name of different states he demanded the nomination of FDR. The public address system, it turned out, was defective. The appeal, grossly distorted and magnified, was dubbed the "voice from the sewer."

Demonstrators may be voting delegates, hired troops, or volunteers brought in for the occasion. The Democrats in 1960 had limited each candidate to 125 outside demonstrators. But when Adlai Stevenson's name was proclaimed from the rostrum, several times that number of marchers appeared. They looked like volunteers eager to do or die for their beloved Adlai. By some slight of hand, apparently, the 125 tickets were used to admit a few hundred paraders to the convention floor.

While the marchers—some costumed, some in mufti—chant and howl for their boy, the accompanying bands pound the air with ear-shattering music. On and on it goes, while the chairman bangs his gavel and begs the demonstrators to take their seats, because the allotted time—now about ten minutes—is used up. The chairman's plea is usually lost in the uproar. Many a gavel has been smashed as the helpless chairman appealed for order. Eventually the demonstrators clear the aisles and the business of the convention is resumed.

The time has now come for the seconding speeches. These are supposed to be held to a ten-minute limit. Each candidate, at least each prominent candidate, may be seconded by three or four, or half a dozen speakers. Somehow, candidates seem to feel that the more seconding speeches, the better the chances of winning the nomination. Usually a candidate calls on seconders from different regions and different social and economic classes. This is designed to give a universal flavor to his candidacy. He is made to appear as a candidate with national appeal. A southern candidate, Lyndon Johnson, was seconded in 1960 by a senator from Connecticut, and by a one-armed World War II hero, a Hawaiian of Japanese descent. This, hopefully, would prove to the delegates and to the nation that Johnson was not just the candidate of a region, but a man with solid support from different classes in broad sections of the country.

By the time the second or third demonstration has been held, it is clear to the searching eye that some of the marchers have appeared before. Among them are mercenaries doing a service for pay. They change their garb as necessary, performing with surface enthusiasm for several candidates in turn. But these are only part of the demonstrators. The others are seriously working for a particular candidate. They may believe that he is the best man in the country for the presidential office or they may have been ordered by their local boss to give their all.

Here and there among the uninhibited, chanting demonstrators are a few surprises—dignified lawmakers and their wives, leaders in government, diplomacy, business, and politics. Marching, singing, and shouting with all the others, they weave their way through aisles and passageways in an endless procession. Panting and puffing, the paraders quit only when the frustrated chairman warns that he'll start the seconding speeches in spite of the noise. Or he may threaten to adjourn the convention. Even this is sometimes insufficient to slow down a demonstration.

As part of the show, balloons may be sent up, to vanish in the upper reaches of the hall. Even doves have been set loose in a heroic effort to add novelty to the proceedings. At the 1948 Democratic convention a lady Democrat presented President Truman, just renominated, with a reproduction of the Liberty Bell, made of flowers. As she told Mr. Truman that the nation expected him to give our nation "peace for all time," she released forty-eight white doves from a basket on the platform. The frightened birds fluttered wildly around the hall and up to the rafters. While most were caught, others continued to swoop and dive all through the acceptance speeches of President Truman and vice presidential candidate Alben Barkley.

It has been mentioned that much convention business takes place in hotel rooms as well as in side rooms of the convention hall and in clusters of delegates and promoters who keep up a continuous buzz on the convention floor. This is inevitable and should not surprise anybody. No group of three thousand delegates, each feeling he may be making history, could be expected to act otherwise. The pressure on these people is intense. Every aspiring candidate tries to capture as many delegates as possible. His assistants and managers work with him, perhaps around the clock, foraging for votes.

The large number of delegates means that many meetings —informal or organized, some planned, some spontaneous— will be taking place at the same time. Delegates are constantly being courted, cajoled, persuaded, or maybe threatened with political exile if they don't back the hottest name. Some delegates are implored to swing a certain way, not on the first ballot, but only on the second or third, when the top contenders may have killed each other off.

Some state delegations, especially in the Democratic party, observe the unit rule. This means that the majority decides how the group shall vote. In other delegations each member votes as an individual. The vote on any ballot may be split two or more ways. A member who questions the arithmetic of his delegation leader may call for a public count of the delegates' vote on the convention floor. Such polling may take place because a delegate sincerely believes an error has been made. Or he may use the poll to stall the convention proceedings. It is possible for one candidate's steamroller to be stopped by this tactic while somebody else's is being revved up for a speedy advance.

To be in the middle of all this is to see what has been called a tawdry show—a spectacle of wheeling and dealing that is unbecoming to a democracy. A hundred years ago a prominent journalist labeled the convention "a system of swindling" the people. A party convention, it is said, should rise to a higher level of honesty, of dignity, of decorum.

But are the convention goings-on really so bad? Three thousand accredited delegates must come up with a name that is satisfactory to the convention, to the party, and to the voters. They must agree on a candidate who will appeal to a cross section of the nation, who can be entrusted with the destiny of the United States and the welfare of his party. How else, except through endless negotiating can a consensus be reached? Politics, after all, can be no more elevated than the people who engage in it and the purpose it serves. The purpose of a nominating convention is to get a few thousand separate, independent individuals—above average in intelligence, in social and economic accomplishment—to reach an agreement that is reasonably acceptable to all. This means discussion, debate, give-and-take. Out of it all must come a name that the party can put before the country with pride and confidence. And this must be done by delegates who talk and argue but who refrain from stabbing or shooting each other.

A disciplined, orderly convention, free of the strenuous politicking that takes place at many American conventions, will probably never happen. Delegates from separate regions, having different interests, may be expected to disagree, to fight. Then, hopefully, differences are composed and the group closes ranks behind a single presidential choice.

It is a sobering fact that the best behaved political meetings probably take place in totalitarian countries. A session of the Supreme Soviet in Russia is a model of rigorous conduct. But its discipline derives not from the consent of free men but from the iron will of a ruthless party machine that nobody dares to challenge. Would any believer in democracy be willing to trade this quiet and order for the noise and confusion of an American nominating convention?

There is no guarantee, of course, that the American-style convention will produce good candidates. Some of the men who have survived the trial of a party convention to win the nomination and the Presidency have not brought honor to their party. Ulysses S. Grant was one. Warren G. Harding was another. But experts in government have repeatedly shown that the men who emerge from the convention to win the Presidency compare favorably with the elected rulers of other countries. Matching British Prime Ministers with American Presidents reveals clearly that our method of electing a President needs no apology.

Harding's nomination was probably the least fortunate result in the history of the nominating process. A combination of circumstances brought about his unexpected victory

at the Republican convention of 1920 in Chicago. At the
time Harding was an obscure United States Senator from
Ohio with minor standing in the party and in the nation. He
was a party hack in the low-level Republican Ohio organization and had won a place in the United States Senate by
doing the bidding of his political overlords. He and his wife
had justified fears about moving into the presidential arena.
In their hearts they knew that he had neither the record, the
ability, nor the moral strength to play the presidential game.
All that could be said in his favor was that he looked like a
President—impressively handsome and distinguished—and
that he had no enemies.

But the ominous decision of 1920 was made not by Harding but for him. The Republican party's leading candidates,
General Leonard Wood and Governor Frank Lowden, stood
each other off at the convention in mortal deadlock. Neither
could garner the votes to win and neither would yield to the
other. This kind of bitterness between big contenders is a
well-known fact of politics, and of life. It happens often
that two candidates and their backers grow so intense about
each other that though neither can win the prize for himself, he cannot tolerate a victory by the other.

In such circumstances the 1920 Republican convention
gave its ear to the promoters of Senator Warren G. Harding.
Contrary to what many people thought, Harding was not
altogether a dark horse. His candidacy had been nurtured
for a long time by his Ohio friends, who came increasingly
to be known as the Ohio gang. Harding's own estimate of his
presidential chances was low. Hours before he was nominated, he filed papers with the Ohio secretary of state to
qualify as a candidate for another term as United States
Senator from Ohio. He made the deadline by a few minutes.

One of Harding's pals, Harry Dougherty, had been work-
ing steadily to make his senator friend a President. Before the
Ohio presidential primary election, campaign manager
Dougherty had been beating the drums for Senator Harding.

In a prophecy that is chilling in its accuracy, Dougherty at that time said, "At the proper time after the Republican National Convention meets, some fifteen men, bleary-eyed with loss of sleep and perspiring profusely with the excessive heat, will sit down in seclusion around a big table. I will be with them and will present the name of Senator Harding to them, and before we get through they will put him over."

This, precisely, is what happened. At one point it became evident to General Wood and to Governor Lowden, and to the whole Republican convention that neither contender could win the nomination. It was now the turn for the manipulators of Warren G. Harding to take command. This they did. In a smoke-filled room at Chicago's Blackstone Hotel, they brought to the big chiefs of the Republican party the name of Warren G. Harding and won agreement that he was to get the presidential nomination. This unhappy decision started a chain of events that ruined a President, besmirched a great political party, and scandalized a nation. Public affairs during Mr. Harding's Presidency dipped to the lowest level in American history.

The odor of that smoke-filled room lingers yet. It became a lasting symbol of dishonest politics, of a group of political fixers secretly making decisions that should be made in public.

By ironic circumstance the notorious smoke-filled room in the Blackstone Hotel briefly hit the newspapers in the 1960 Republican convention at Chicago. Richard Nixon, the unchallenged leader for the Republican nomination in that year, learned with dismay that he had been assigned the same room that had figured in the 1920 campaign. The Vice President backed away from any association with the Harding tradition and insisted on having different accommodations.

The matter of a smoke-filled room is not important, but some things are important: the character of the proceedings, the quality of the people who do the negotiating, the caliber of the man they decide to support, and above all whether the delegates are free men who are able to vote their own convictions when the balloting begins.

Smoke-filled rooms and smoke-filled convention halls are part of the nomination picture. There is nothing inherently evil in a smoke-filled room and we may assume that this will continue to be a permanent aspect of conventions. There is reassurance in the fact that with or without the smoke, the conventions have generally produced candidates who have borne their presidential responsibilities with credit if not with nobility.

Harry Dougherty's kingmaker role in the 1920 Republican convention was odious but not unfamiliar. This breed is well known in American politics. Never, though, have the results of kingmaking been as bad as in the scandal-pocked administration of Warren G. Harding.

Many men have tried for the role of kingmaker, preferring to use their behind-scene power to create a President, rather than compete for high office themselves. Mark Hanna was kingmaker to William McKinley in 1896. Without Hanna's money and determination McKinley would surely not have reached the Presidency. Yet McKinley gave a better-than-average performance as President.

Presidents who are about to leave office have sometimes played the part of kingmaker by easing the path for a chosen successor. It is doubtful whether Martin Van Buren could have made it without Andrew Jackson's energetic help in 1836. Similarly it took the power and prestige of Theodore Roosevelt to make William Howard Taft a President in 1908.

Some men would like to be kingmakers, but lack the strength such a part requires. Many of them have to settle for the illusion that their support put the candidate across. In the 1960 Democratic election, at least a dozen political leaders were called kingmakers or felt they deserved the title.

The fact is that John F. Kennedy made himself President by driving himself and his dedicated team to the limits of human endurance.

Usually a President in office can be re-elected because he controls the party machinery. But this is not always easy. In 1948, Democratic prospects were dark. President Truman was urged by some jittery Democrats to save the party by personally nominating General Eisenhower as the Democratic candidate. But at this time the general was not willing to talk politics. A reluctant Democratic convention thereupon nominated Mr. Truman for a full term. He surprised and delighted his party by the combative spirit he put into the campaign. And he brought about one of the great upsets in presidential history in his final victory over Tom Dewey.

Once the convention delegates have resolved the great issue, naming a candidate, the rest is anticlimax. In recent years, following the example of Franklin Roosevelt, the victorious nominee has appeared before the convention to accept the nomination without waiting to be formally notified of his success.

The convention then turns to one of its final tasks—selecting a vice presidential candidate. More and more the successful candidate for President decides who shall be his running mate. Though the choice may appear to be open, the presidential nominee usually picks the candidate for Vice President. One exception was the 1956 Democratic convention. Adlai Stevenson, having been nominated for President, said he wanted the convention itself to name the vice presidential candidate.

In the open contest that followed, John F. Kennedy was nosed out by Estes Kefauver, whose name was then added to Stevenson's on the Democratic ticket. In the 1960 conventions, candidates Richard Nixon and John F. Kennedy both asserted their full power to pick their teammates.

The Vice Presidency has long been regarded as a political graveyard. John Adams, the first Vice President, defined the job in words that have stuck. It was, he said, "the most insignificant office that ever the invention of man contrived or his imagination conceived." In 1900 Theodore Roosevelt resisted the vice presidential honor that was pressed on him by party chiefs who wanted to get him out of the governorship of New York. He considered the Vice Presidency the end of the line, politically, and perhaps it was. But President William McKinley was assassinated and Theodore Roosevelt inherited the Presidency itself.

Altogether seven American Presidents have died in office. This grim fact proves the seriousness of the choice of vice presidential candidates. It means that the conventions should name for Vice President only men who are big enough to be President. This was the clear intention of the Founding Fathers, who asked in the Constitution that two men be named by the electors; the one with the highest number of votes would be President, the other Vice President. But both were to be "continental characters," men of substance, wisdom, and experience.

Convention delegates have not always filled this responsibility with the sober care it requires. By the time they reach this part of their business the delegates are usually tired and harassed and eager to go home. They have sometimes seemed ready to name almost anybody to the job so the convention could adjourn.

In 1940 the Republicans paired Wendell Willkie with a man he had never met before, Charles McNary. Their views on public power projects—a big issue—were completely opposed. The 1884 Republican ticket of Blaine and Logan was stranger still. These two men hated each other yet they ran as a team. Logan's feeling toward Blaine was summarized in a popular couplet of the day:

> We never speak as we pass by,
> Me to Jim Blaine nor him to I.

In recent years, especially since Henry Wallace went on

the ballot with Franklin Roosevelt in 1940, the job has become more important. President Truman widened the responsibilities of Vice President Alben Barkley. President Eisenhower gave new powers to Vice President Nixon during the two terms of 1953-1961. Little is heard now about the Vice Presidency being a ticket to oblivion. Mr. Nixon proved in 1960 that a Vice President might become the unchallenged claimant for the presidential nomination.

The competition for the Vice Presidency has in recent years been vigorous. In 1940 it took all the prestige and influence of President Roosevelt to get Henry Wallace nominated as Vice President. So bitter was the feeling against Wallace on the convention floor that he was not permitted to deliver his acceptance speech. Four years later the opponents of Wallace—chiefly conservatives from the South, and big-city political bosses—ditched him altogether, even though Mr. Roosevelt seemed to prefer him as a running mate.

In general the Vice Presidency is used by the presidential nominee to pacify dissatisfied groups in the party. In this spirit Mr. Roosevelt took Harry Truman on his ticket in 1944. Or the Vice Presidency may be used to balance the ticket geographically. A presidential candidate from an eastern, industrialized area may favor a westerner or southerner to run with him. Sometimes an aspirant for the presidential nomination will dangle vice presidential bait before important convention leaders in return for their support. John F. Kennedy's lieutenants in 1960 enticed several Democratic chieftains into his camp by hints of a big reward—the Vice Presidency. As the history books show, none of them got it.

In the 1932 convention Franklin Roosevelt, the liberal front-runner from New York, needed votes to go over the top. He got them from Texas and California by accepting conservative Texan John Garner as his running mate.

Republican Richard Nixon tried hard to get Governor

Nelson Rockefeller of New York to team up with him in 1960. This would have given Nixon, a Californian, all the ingredients he felt necessary for success. Rockefeller was an outstanding eastern liberal with proved vote-getting ability. He appealed strongly to a big slice of the voting public who were cool to Nixon. Together they couldn't miss. But Rockefeller resisted intense pressure to run for Vice President. He wanted top place on the ticket or nothing. Nixon had to settle for Henry Cabot Lodge, who eagerly accepted the honor.

In 1960 John F. Kennedy of Boston astounded the Chicago Democratic convention by picking Senator Lyndon Johnson of Texas as teammate. Johnson was considered an unlikely prospect for a liberal team running on a liberal platform. It was felt that as a southerner, Johnson was only lukewarm on civil rights and he was hardly an intimate friend of the big labor leaders. On these grounds alone, it would seem, Johnson was ruled out. But there was more. Both before and during the Democratic convention, Johnson had attacked Senator Kennedy repeatedly—for his frequent absence from the Senate, for his wealth, for his youth, for his father's political record.

Why did Kennedy offer the Vice Presidency to his hard-hitting rival? Because Texan Johnson could offer geographic balance to the ticket; because Johnson could perhaps hold the southern voters in line for the Democratic party; because the convention had adopted a strong civil rights platform that might touch off a southern revolt. Only a popular, appealing southerner like Johnson might dampen the fires of rebellion. In short, Kennedy figured that he needed Johnson more, say, than he needed Senator Hubert Humphrey of Minnesota. Humphrey was a strong liberal who appealed to workers, to city folks, to intellectuals, to Negroes. Kennedy believed he already had the support of these groups. He wanted to be sure of his southern anchor.

Many southern Democrats disliked the civil rights parts

of the platform. They felt that organized labor was already too strong in the party. They objected to portions of the platform that promised greater expenditures for education, housing, social security, health. In Kennedy's judgment only a southerner, respected by other southerners, could deliver the South for the Democratic party. And without the South the Democratic candidate could not win.

The rest is history. No candidate for President ever calculated more shrewdly or more accurately. Lyndon Johnson performed his assigned role with great skill. The team of Kennedy and Johnson prevailed—by the thinnest margin, less than two-tenths of one per cent—over the Republican pair, Nixon and Lodge.

Folks on the sidelines wondered why Johnson accepted second place on the ticket. Wasn't he too big for the job? Wasn't he more important as Senate majority leader than a Vice President could ever hope to be? There were answers. Some felt that Johnson decided that Vice Presidents have a bigger place in history books than Senate majority leaders. Others noted that two four-year terms as Vice President could give Johnson the inside track for the presidential nomination in 1968. Most people believed that Johnson was not the sort of man who would vegetate in the vice presidential office. He would expect—and he would receive—powers and responsibilities that fitted his ability and energy. He would make the Vice Presidency an important, headline-winning office because that's the way he operated.

Once the Vice President has been agreed upon, the nominating convention has two tasks to complete. One is to select a new national committee. From each state delegation a man and woman are named. This new committee rules the destiny of the party for the next four years. It also selects as national chairman the man who has been tapped by the presidential nominee.

The convention then goes through its ceremonial closing. In this ritual the defeated candidates ask all party members to dedicate themselves to presidential victory under their chosen leaders. The candidates for President and Vice President forecast the issues on which they will campaign for office. In his speech before 70,000 listeners assembled at the Los Angeles Coliseum on the closing day of the 1960 Democratic convention, John F. Kennedy called for a New Frontier for America—a frontier of greater democratic rights for Americans and for all people, a frontier of hard work and sacrifice that might achieve peace and security for ourselves and for our world neighbors.

The curtain came down on another quadrennial national nominating convention. The campaign was now started for the Presidency of the United States.

CHAPTER FIVE

THE CAMPAIGN

THE MORNING AFTER ELECTION DAY, 1960, JOHN F. KENNEDY, under the eye of the newly assigned Secret Service, walked the hundred yards from his home in Hyannisport, Massachusetts, to the house of his brother Robert. Here were gathered the people who had led John Kennedy's long, exhausting, and victorious presidential campaign. These were the men with whom he had lived and worked for many months—at headquarters and at hotels, on planes and trains, at meetings and rallies and demonstrations, in fair weather and foul. As John Kennedy strode into his brother's living room these people, for the first time, rose at his appearance. Now they greeted not their familiar boss Jack, but the President-elect of the United States.

This episode symbolized the mighty transformation that had taken place overnight. John Kennedy was no longer the hungry candidate, pursuing every last voter wherever he might be found—at factory gate or Main Street, at a town hall rally or in a high school auditorium or at home before his television set. All that was over. Mr. Kennedy was now President-to-be.

What route had Mr. Kennedy traveled to reach his cherished goal? What had he done between the time he won his party's nomination and that day in November when the voters decided the issue? What happens in the battle that begins when the two nominating conventions end?

In some ways, presidential campaigns have been the same for most of our history. Every four years, usually on a hot night in early summer, the two major parties name their standard bearer in big nominating conventions. During late summer and early fall the candidates go before the American people to plead their case. Some candidates—Abraham Lincoln, Ulysses S. Grant, William McKinley, for example—stayed at home and let their lieutenants go forth to win the people's votes. These candidates thought it inappropriate to solicit votes in person. Lincoln felt that canvassing for votes was beneath presidential dignity. Gradually this taboo vanished. Only Presidents in office who were seeking a second term felt restrained from hitting the campaign trail. But this inhibition, too, has worn thin. In our day a President who wants to be re-elected goes before the people and says so. Presidents William Howard Taft, Woodrow Wilson, Herbert Hoover, Franklin Roosevelt, Harry Truman, and Dwight Eisenhower campaigned for their own re-election while they were in the Chief Executive's office.

In the twentieth century the pace of the presidential campaign has been greatly stepped up. Radio, television, and the airplane have made the whole nation a potential audience for campaign orators. But the revolutionary changes in communication and travel have not made campaigning easier. On the contrary, they've made it more bruising and more taxing than ever.

Back in Andrew Jackson's day, the torchlight parade was the big thrill of the political season in many a town. The torch-bearing demonstrators might number anywhere from a few hundred to thousands. Sometimes the drama was intensified by the candidate's personal appearance. For half a century the torchlight parade remained a staple of the presidential contest.

The political rally was another favorite of campaign managers. They arranged for their candidate to address a host of community gatherings. In some villages the rally was the event of the year. Townspeople and countryfolk joined in preparations to make it a social as well as political event. It sometimes took on the flavor of a fair, with a touch of carnival added. The arrival of the presidential candidate signaled the start of the grand procession to the exhibition or ball grounds.

The high point of the rally was the candidate's speech. This was usually a one-shot opportunity for him to win voters to his cause. Inasmuch as he would probably not return for a second appearance, he had to make good in this single effort. He could be counted on to give a well-rehearsed, memorized talk. In the days before radio, a candidate needed only two or three set speeches to carry him through a campaign. There was just limited press coverage, so the candidate could endlessly repeat his ideas in the same words and not worry about it. The speech could be the same because the audience was always different.

A major change in campaigning came with the greater use of the railroad. This made it possible for the candidate to put real mileage into his quest for votes. The heaviest user of railroads in the turn-of-the-century period was William Jennings Bryan, who began his long, futile pursuit of the Presidency in 1896 against William McKinley. Bryan threw himself into campaigning with a zeal that amazed his friends and appalled his enemies. Riding his "campaign special," he seemed able to give unlimited speeches. Bryan made an art of the short political talk delivered at obscure villages and unheard-of "whistle stops." In his 1900 race with McKinley, Bryan logged six hundred speeches in twenty-four states in three months.

Perhaps the last great practitioner of the whistle-stop tour was Harry Truman, who in 1948 surprised the nation by the vigor of his campaign and his unexpected victory. Always at his best in off-the-cuff oratory, Truman found the whistle-stop tour perfectly suited to his talents. He didn't weary of the endless train stops and rear-platform speeches. He was freshened and buoyed by the exchange of greetings with clusters of American voters at railroad crossings, big and little. In his 1948 tour he covered over 30,000 miles and delivered over five hundred speeches. He relished the audience's cry to "Give 'em hell, Harry," and this is exactly what he did, heaping brimstone and fire on the Republican enemy.

After he completed his own Presidency, Mr. Truman made his services available to the Democratic candidates who succeeded him—Stevenson in 1952 and 1956, and Kennedy in 1960. In fact, Mr. Truman's attacks on the Republican candidate sometimes embarrassed Democratic headquarters. But this did not discourage the energetic former President. He stood ready, if his party needed him, to board a train for still another whistle-stop tour.

In 1932 for the first time, the airplane came onto the campaign scene. Franklin Roosevelt flew from Albany to Chicago to accept the nomination of the Democratic presidential convention in person. Previous nominees had waited for an official committee to call on them with the good news. FDR broke this tradition and at the same time made the airplane a vehicle for presidential campaigning.

But even in the 1960 campaign the railroads still played a part. Though the candidates traveled much by air, they learned that an airport is not the happiest setting for a campaign speech. It is usually miles out of town and therefore not a natural rallying-place for the needed welcoming crowds. Local politicians, who want to be photographed with the presidential candidate and spend some time with him, are put into an awkward spot when they join the air caravan. In a short time they may be miles from where they started, and faced with unwelcome expense and loss of time in getting back home. Nevertheless, plane travel—the "prop" stop—has in large measure replaced the whistle stop.

The candidate who can afford to campaign by air has a sizeable advantage. In the 1960 Democratic primaries, airborne candidate John Kennedy out-traveled and out-paced his chief rival, Hubert Humphrey, who couldn't afford an air operation. Humphrey, dependent on commercial planes, had to time his appearances to conform to the airline schedule. Part of the time, Humphrey relied on a private bus, a pathetic substitute for Mr. Kennedy's private plane. Nevertheless the hazards of weather and the heavy cost of airborne campaigns suggest that the railroad and the whistle stop will continue to be at least a minor feature of presidential campaigns.

In 1924, for the first time, the voices of presidential candidates went on the air. The semi-private speech to small groups of citizens all over the country was supplanted by the radio hookup and the radio network. Microphones and a tangle of cables and wire became a familiar part of campaign scenery. Folksy chit-chat tended to give way to the more carefully prepared address. Candidates now had to remember that their words were reaching listeners far removed from the local audience. The unskilled speaker was put at an ever-greater disadvantage. Alf Landon, the 1936 Republican opponent of Franklin Roosevelt, was sadly outclassed as an orator. When he was introduced to an audience, apologies were sometimes made for his lack of brilliance on the platform. Only his devoted followers could sit through his performance, a fact that contributed to his disaster on election day.

By 1952 television had become a big factor in the search for votes. Candidates for presidential office had to have not only a voice but the face to go with it. Probably neither party today would put up a candidate who lacked the ability to speak reasonably well. And the party leaders would probably insist that a candidate must also register effectively on the television screen.

It has already been mentioned that John Kennedy, as a result of his 1960 television debates with Richard Nixon, moved forward in the presidential race. Kennedy was sure he could do this. When he was asked, early in the campaign, how he expected to win, he readily answered, "In the debates." Nobody doubts that the image delivered on the TV screen helps people decide how to vote. By the time the four Kennedy-Nixon debates were finished, the picture was clear to a majority of Americans—John Kennedy could be trusted with the Presidency.

The campaign is climaxed, of course, on election day. As votes are tallied, the nation holds its breath, and relaxes only when the winner is announced. The new President-elect is immediately enveloped by Secret Service men who guard him around the clock. At the same moment, the victor becomes wrapped in the mantle of greatness that goes with the American Presidency. Not every President has proved equal to the job's dimensions. But people's expectations are high, and their idea of the Presidency is an exalted one. Some Presidents who looked a bit undersized at first began to grow when they started on the job. Such Presidents have included Chester A. Arthur and Harry Truman, who showed unexpected ability and courage in the presidential office.

To some degree, a similar change comes over a man when he wins his party's nomination for the Presidency. Before this decision is reached, he may be just one among several politicians grappling for the prized nomination.

Until the nominating conventions make their choice, the eager competitors race around the country trying to win primaries and to capture delegates to the nominating convention. As they pursue these exalted vote-holders, the aspirants say things about each other that are unflattering and sometimes slanderous. The pre-convention fight may get so venomous, that it is hard to believe the antagonists are leaders in the same party. Would-be candidates and their supporters may inflict wounds that cannot heal in the months after the convention. Even a famous friendship like that of Al Smith and Franklin Roosevelt back in the 1920's may be a convention-time casualty. These men were fond of each other and both were unshakeably loyal to their party. But after FDR won the 1932 Democratic nomination, he and Al Smith became estranged and were never reconciled.

In 1960, however, John F. Kennedy succeeded in getting his rivals and opponents together immediately after he won the nomination. Among the Democratic leaders who had opposed Mr. Kennedy were former President Truman, Mrs. Eleanor Roosevelt, Senator Stuart Symington, Adlai Stevenson, Senator Hubert Humphrey, and Senator Lyndon Johnson. Yet John Kennedy hauled them all aboard the Kennedy bandwagon. Most of them appeared with him at the Los Angeles Coliseum when he came forward to accept his party's nomination. They spoke for him and worked for him in the strenuous campaign that got under way that very night.

Governor Robert Meyner, New Jersey's favorite son who had held out for his own nomination at the 1960 Democratic convention, took charge of the Kennedy campaign in New Jersey. The governor accompanied the candidate on a state-wide tour. The New Jersey Democratic machine, with Meyner in the driver's seat, rolled in high gear right up to election day. New Jersey voters watching Governor Meyner introduce candidate Kennedy could only point to Meyner and sigh, "There, but for the grace of God, goes our next President." And so it might have been. A different deal of the political cards might have made Robert Meyner—or any of a half dozen others—the Democratic candidate for President. John Kennedy would then have been the solicitous escort, instead of the star attraction.

Students of American politics were impressed by the thoroughness and the strength of the Kennedy organization.

Some referred to the Kennedy tactics as blitz or lightning when they described how he took the Democratic nomination at Los Angeles in 1960. Never had they seen such careful preparation, such attention to detail, or such power concentrated on a single aim—to win the nomination.

John Kennedy's campaign, of course, had begun four years earlier when he barely missed the 1956 Democratic vice presidential nomination. He began then to put together a political machine that could give him the Democratic nomination in 1960. As a student of presidential politics he knew well the size of the job ahead. But he had the brains, the ambition, and—very important—the money to weld a powerful machine. He determined to take every action that might bring him to his goal.

Presidential campaigns have not always been so well organized. Before the days of Franklin Roosevelt, a great deal was left to chance or to intuition. Much politicking was done on a personal and informal basis. This was true in the scramble to win the party nomination as well as in the election race itself. There were big gaps in the organizational plans of both parties. Neither side tried to reach all the voters in all the states. The pace of campaigning was more leisurely than today.

Republican Mark Hanna, who ran William McKinley's campaign in 1896 and 1900, bore down on wealthy party members to fill his war chest. Hanna believed he could put his man across without any elaborate campaigning if only he had ample funds. McKinley himself stayed home and received groups of visitors informally during the campaign. He was confident that Hanna's strategy would work and, of course, it did.

The campaign of Franklin Roosevelt in 1932 was different. Under Jim Farley's management, the Democratic candidate reached more people than any man before him. Farley brought new efficiency and power into the presidential campaign. He had records of who was who, politically, all over the nation. He made it his business to sell his candidate to every party leader he could reach. Farley was widely known and respected, and at the critical moment at the convention he was able to cash in all the promises of his political friends.

Presidential politics was never the same after 1932. From that date every candidate for the Presidency has known that in order to win he needs a campaign apparatus that reaches into the remote parts of the country. This means that well before the convention, each aspirant should try to build a political machine that can win him the nomination and then carry him to victory on election day.

All candidates, Democratic and Republican alike, know that the pursuit of the Presidency is a rough game. It calls for never-draining toil, for pushing the human body to the breaking point. Abraham Lincoln once spoke of an election he had lost. He felt, said Lincoln, like a little boy who had stubbed his toe in the dark. He was too old to cry, but it hurt too much to laugh. Adlai Stevenson, who tried for the Presidency in 1952 and 1956, said that campaigning was like trying to punch holes in a fog.

Some would-be Presidents do not have the inclination, or the funds, or the stomach for this kind of contest. Some would like to be drafted for the Presidency by a nominating convention that sees their virtues shining through the political fog that hangs over the convention hall. This is possible, of course. Willkie in 1940, and both Eisenhower and Stevenson in 1952, captured their party nominations though they lacked the elaborate, pre-convention organizations of some of their competitors. But the chance of this happening grows slimmer all the time. Political fortune favors the man who rides into the convention city aboard a well-greased, fast-rolling political machine.

No man has ever prepared for victory like John F. Kennedy. The methods and the labors of other would-be candidates in both parties pale by comparison with Kennedy's.

He planned two separate operations—one to win the nomination and a second to win the election. This two-stage assault is usually necessary in a presidential election.

Sometimes a candidate may be spared the pre-convention fight. If, for example, a President in office is running for another term, he usually has no opposition for the nomination. Or if the President throws his official support to one candidate, this, too, makes a difference. In 1960 President Eisenhower named Richard Nixon as his heir. Nixon entered the Republican convention with the sure knowledge that he would take the nomination.

Kennedy won his two campaigns by dogged, man-killing work. He fine-combed the nation for delegates who would stand with him at the Los Angeles convention. He did it all over again to win the people's support on election day.

After the Democratic convention had made John Kennedy their choice, brother Robert Kennedy told what had to be done to win the election in November. "We're trying to get an organization going that is bigger than United States Steel, and we're trying to do it in three months." This was a good comparison. Within a short time the Kennedy table of organization looked like the plan for a big military operation. A "Kennedy Organization Manual" told every state and local Kennedy worker just what to do and how to do it: how to multiply the working staff, how to run a Kennedy rally, how to manage mass telephone calls that would bring out the voters.

The Kennedy strategy board signed up an astonishing array of campaign talent. It was a mixed bag of workers that included intellectuals—eggheads—and the most hardheaded of professional politicians. There were relatives, friends and classmates, fellow members of Congress, and old Navy cronies, all ready to give their all for JFK. There was a host of specialists, each with some particular skill that could help the Kennedy cause. These included historians, economists, lawyers, scientific advisers, communications and transportation specialists, publicity and advertising experts, advance men, accountants, and jacks-of-all-trades.

Why did Mr. Kennedy require such a variety of costly talent? Because campaigning in our time is a complicated operation. Specialists are needed to handle the many tasks that go into a successful campaign. A candidate with good speech material, good looks, and a good voice won't win votes if a slip-up in transportation puts him in one town while his audience is waiting in another. This can happen and has happened.

What about the other specialists mentioned above? Both candidates in 1960 needed speech writers, researchers, and authorities on domestic and foreign problems. The candidates had to be sure that their speeches were meaty, accurate, and interesting. They couldn't possibly spend the necessary hours pulling information together and whipping it into good speech material. Trained, qualified experts had to do the job for them. Both candidates wanted to be sure they sounded good on radio and looked good on television. Each depended on skilled technicians to project his voice and his looks in a way that would win votes.

A separate arm of the campaign organization took care of finances. More will be said about this later. But it is obvious that the available money had to be spent where it would do the most good. This required the full-time labor of financial experts assisted by competent staff.

One of the unusual features of the Kennedy campaign was the assignment of trained workers to ferret out unregistered voters. This special squad fanned out over the country to sign up unregistered citizens so they could vote in the November election. This project was headed by Congressman Frank Thompson, a strong Kennedy supporter. The organization included fifty state registration chairmen and a similar chairman in each of two hundred important counties in the nation.

The leg work was done by 200,000 recruiters who scoured the towns and villages and cities—including the neglected upper floors of tenements—in a vast hunt for the forgotten voter. The Kennedy leaders believed that most of these people, if they could be made to register and then to vote, would support the Democratic nominee. Many of these potential voters were foreign-born or Negroes. Most were low on the economic scale and had been generally ignored, politically.

The count on election day showed that Kennedy's $200,000 investment in unregistered voters had paid off. In California 140,000 new Spanish-speaking Democrats were corralled into Viva Kennedy Clubs. Across the nation, a few million Americans who formerly had not cared one way or the other about the choice of a President, learned to vote—Democratic.

Another group of Kennedy specialists toured the country to meet with political leaders, to learn about their local and regional problems, and to try to cement their loyalty to Kennedy. Many of these local leaders needed to be convinced that it was to their personal interest to support the Democratic nominee. The election results seemed to justify this special effort to nudge the small-time politicians into action.

The Nixon forces neglected none of these people. Apparently, though, they did not cover the nation as thoroughly or intensively as the Kennedy group. The Nixon team perhaps underestimated the size of the hidden vote. In any case they did not seem to go after it as zealously as the Kennedy men.

Candidates Nixon and Kennedy chided each other about the elaborate, expensive apparatus each used in the 1960 campaign. Much was said about the "Madison Avenue" sell, that is, the coating of charm that was applied to each candidate in order to increase his appeal to the voters. The implication, of course, was that each candidate was made attractive by synthetic means, by slick devices associated with

Madison Avenue, the heart of the advertising world. But Democrats and Republicans alike used skilled publicity men. The sole job of these specialists was to make their candidate look good, and get the voter to pull the right lever when election day rolled around. Both parties used roughly the same variety of experts and the same costly methods in the drive to victory. Probably Mr. Kennedy's machine was more elaborate, more highly charged, and tougher than Mr. Nixon's.

It was generally believed that Senator Kennedy's personal campaign staff in 1960 put in the hardest, longest days ever known to campaign history. His air caravan, with its crowded schedule of stops, often was late. The break for lunch was therefore frequently omitted. At one point in the campaign Senator Kennedy had said that after eight years of Republican rule, seventeen million Americans still suffered from undernourishment. One of Kennedy's overworked, underfed campaign staff remarked to his weary colleagues, "The Senator has said that seventeen million Americans go to bed hungry at night, and he expects you to do your part."

Though the 1960 campaign was tough and bruising, it is certain that tomorrow's presidential contestants will regard the 1960 operation as minimal, and will go on to wage campaigns that are even more intense, more stressful, more taxing.

CHAPTER SIX

THE STUFF OF VICTORY

A PRESIDENTIAL CAMPAIGN IS USUALLY MARKED BY ROUGH IN-fighting. A candidate must be prepared to hear himself maligned, and to see his past resurrected and displayed for public viewing. This may happen even in the primaries, when contestants are fighting for delegates to the national nominating convention. At the convention itself, the would-be candidates may fling charges at each other, right up to the moment that one of them is designated as the party's nominee. After the two parties have made their decision, the Republican and Democratic nominees begin to take each other apart. Each is backed by assistants and researchers and partisans who fuel the campaign and keep it hot.

No topic is too private for public exposure in a campaign. Some accusations are made openly; others are leaked by un-identified sources and circulated in whispering campaigns or anonymous leaflets. The 1928 Hoover-Smith campaign was disgraced by the use of handbills that accused Al Smith of favoring marriage between Negro and white; of being a tool of the Pope; of wanting to make Washington an outpost of Catholic Rome. Similar literature was distributed in 1960 in the effort to frighten voters away from Roman Catholic candidate Kennedy.

The 1884 Blaine-Cleveland contest was enlivened by newspaper stories accusing Democrat Cleveland of being the father of an illegitimate child. Cleveland denied nothing and admitted that he was paying the support of a lady-friend's youngster. The Republicans made all possible use of the issue. In New York they paraded up Fifth Avenue chanting:

Ma, Ma, where's my Pa?

The Democrats organized their own parade and, making a virtue of necessity, replied:

Ma, Ma, where's my Pa?
Gone to the White House, ha, ha, ha!

Democratic strategists had plenty of ammunition against James G. Blaine, the "plumed knight" of the Republican party. Blaine had had a long and famous career in Congress, but there was evidence that he had used his office to profit financially in private business transactions. Back in 1876 he had gone before the House of Representatives to answer the accusations that had been lodged against him. Then, during the 1884 presidential campaign some letters were brought to light that made the candidate look bad all over again. In one of these letters, addressed to a business partner, Blaine made some embarrassing admissions and ended with the words, "Burn this letter." But the partner did not burn the letter. It eventually fell into the hands of a clerk named Mulligan and found its way to Democratic headquarters. The party chieftains pounced on it. The Democrats could now be heard chanting:

Burn this letter! Burn this letter!
Burn, burn, oh burn this letter!

Thomas Nast, one of America's great political cartoonists, went to work in the pages of *Harper's Weekly* to picture Blaine as a grafting, crooked politician. The image of Blaine as dishonest and unfit for the Presidency was spread everywhere. Another chant heard in that campaign ran:

> Blaine, Blaine, James G. Blaine,
> The Continental liar from the State of Maine,
> Burn this letter!

Many a man who relishes the idea of becoming President decides against it because he's unwilling to get into rough combat. In the 1872 campaign, Horace Greeley, editor of the *New York Tribune*, was the Democratic and Liberal-Republican candidate against Ulysses Grant who ran for re-election. While Republican Grant stayed home and made no speeches, Greeley fought hard for public support. As a reformer who promised to clean up after the first Grant administration, Greeley expected all honest Americans to rush to his side. But this didn't happen. While Greeley's campaign slipped badly, Grant's wealthy friends pushed their hero closer to victory. Before election day, Greeley's wife became ill and he stopped campaigning actively. He had counted on the support of Negroes because he had long been their champion. He had been an abolitionist and spokesman for Negro rights for years. His newspaper had also been friendly to the business class and had approved their demand for a high protective tariff. Now, when his Negro and businessmen friends might have repaid him with their votes, they deserted him. The violent campaign attacks—from friend and foe— left him ill. It was hard to tell, he said, whether he was running for "President or the penitentiary." A defeated and saddened man, he died shortly after the election.

Many a candidate has been similarly disillusioned, though few have had Horace Greeley's dismal end. In the 1952 campaign, Eisenhower's running mate, Senator Richard Nixon, suddenly found himself awash in nasty headlines. He was accused of accepting an $18,000 fund put together by wealthy Californians to round out his income as United States Senator from California. The charges were especially embarrassing because Mr. Eisenhower was leading a "crusade" for clean government. What to do? A nervous Nixon, aware that Mr. Eisenhower might drop him as vice presidential candidate, went before the television cameras, and explained everything. He had used the money, he said, so he could do a better job of representing the people of California. The fund had made possible more travel and closer communication between his constitutents on the coast and the government in Washington; none of it had stuck to his own fingers. He then talked about his puppy Checkers, also a gift. Let it be understood, he said, that he was not giving Checkers back. Many a tear dropped as the candidate told his story. Eisenhower embraced his contrite vice presidential candidate, proclaimed him "clean as a hound's tooth" and the campaign rolled on.

No candidate in American history suffered more abuse than William Jennings Bryan, who started running for President in 1896 but never made it. In the first campaign against William McKinley, Bryan learned how disreputable presidential politics can become. Though Bryan was a teetotaler who had no use for liquor in any form, this is what he heard during the campaign:

> McKinley drinks soda water,
> Bryan drinks rum;
> McKinley is a gentleman,
> Bryan is a bum!

That, however, wasn't the worst of it. Workmen at various plants were told by their employers that if Bryan were elected, the factories would close down. Said the head of a big piano company to his workers the day before election, ". . . if Bryan is elected tomorrow the whistle will not blow Wednesday morning." This put a cruel choice to Bryan's working-class friends.

In the 1944 race between Thomas Dewey and Franklin

Roosevelt, the Republicans tried a device that backfired. They charged that Roosevelt, on a wartime inspection tour of the Pacific, had unfortunately left his puppy Fala in the Aleutian Islands. When the President discovered this, said the Republicans, he ordered a United States Navy destroyer to steam to the Aleutians to pick up his dog.

In a campaign speech to the Teamsters Union, President Roosevelt referred to the Fala story. "These Republican leaders," said the President, "have not been content with attacks upon me, or my wife or my sons—they now include my little dog Fala. Unlike the members of my family, he resents this. Being a Scottie, as soon as he learned that the Republican fiction writers had concocted a story that I had left him behind on an Aleutian island and had sent a destroyer back to find him at a cost to the taxpayers of two or three or twenty million dollars, his Scotch soul was furious. He has not been the same dog since."

An explosion of laughs greeted the President's tale. He had succeeded brilliantly in turning attack into counter-attack.

How much damage do candidates inflict on each other in these campaign sorties? This is hard to say. Some accusations go deep, others are mere surface blows. The American public expects that the contestants in a presidential competition will rough each other up. Most people don't get terribly excited by the bloodletting in a campaign. They expect it. But many Americans were nevertheless surprised by a remark once made by Wendell Willkie. When he ran against Franklin Roosevelt in 1940, Willkie had grimly warned that a third term for FDR would clamp a totalitarian dictatorship on the United States. But the next year a defeated but generous-minded Willkie went before a Senate committee to endorse President Roosevelt's defense policies. Willkie was asked how he could support the program of a President whom he had so recently condemned as a would-be dictator. With his disarming smile Willkie answered, "Occasionally in moments of oratory we all expand a little bit."

Every candidate in a presidential contest reaches for the immortal slogan—some happy combination of words that will stick in the public mind and help his candidacy. Once in a while a candidate strikes it rich and finds words that are exactly right for the times. Such a phrase was the "New Deal" that Franklin Roosevelt promised the American people in 1932. He followed it up in his first inaugural speech by saying, "The only thing we have to fear is fear itself." To a nation racked by troubles—unemployment, hunger, stagnation, bleak insecurity—the words had a jolting effect. A heavy-hearted people looked up and wondered, could there really be a brighter tomorrow? Few phrases in America's political dictionary have penetrated so deep or been so much quoted.

Ulysses S. Grant, the hero of the Civil War, touched the right chord in the 1868 campaign when he said simply, "Let us have peace." A war-tired people warmed to this appealing sentiment.

Sometimes a casual expression is turned to political use with deadly results. Such an episode took place in the 1884 battle between Democrat Grover Cleveland and Republican James G. Blaine. Cleveland, who was believed by some voters to be both anti-labor and anti-Catholic, was given only a slim chance of winning. At the end of October, 1884, a few days before the election, Blaine returned to New York after an exhausting tour of the West. The candidate was greeted by a delegation of Protestant ministers who wanted to assure him of their support. One of them, a Mr. Burchard, told Blaine that the ministers were solidly for him, and would have nothing to do with Cleveland's Democrats. The clergymen, said Burchard, would not abandon the Republican party and "identify ourselves with the party of Rum, Romanism and Rebellion. We are loyal to our flag. We are loyal to you." A tired Mr. Blaine either did not hear or did not catch the meaning of this remark that labeled the Democrats as drinkers, as Roman Catholics, as disloyal Americans. But some Democrats did hear it and they knew an issue when they saw it. They picked up the phrase "Rum, Romanism, and Rebellion," and let the word go out that this was Blaine's opinion of the Democrats.

The Irish, the Catholics, and the Democrats generally, were stung by the slogan and rallied to Cleveland. The Democratic candidate won in New York by exactly 1149 popular—and crucial—votes. Blaine could only lament the visit to him of what he called "an ass in the shape of a preacher."

McKinley's phrasemakers had trouble finding something to rhyme with "McKinley." But they did come up with the thought that McKinley was "the advance agent of prosperity," and this was a pleasant prospect. They also assured the public that McKinley's election meant a "full dinner pail." This phrase, too, registered well.

The same idea was put to work for Herbert Hoover in his 1928 race with Al Smith. His election, promised Hoover, would mean "a chicken in every pot and a car in every garage." By the end of his term the nation's economy was in sad shape, with the number of hungry, jobless workers growing steadily. So in the 1932 election the Democrats taunted Hoover with his 1928 promise and explained "Now our families have no chicken and no car; besides they've had to move into the garage."

Woodrow Wilson benefited from the slogan, "He kept us out of war" when he ran for re-election in 1916. People took it as a promise that this country would stay out of the European conflict though it soon turned out otherwise. After the war, Warren G. Harding pledged the American people he would lead them "back to normalcy." This sounded like merciful relief from the burdens, the sacrifice, and the responsibilities they associated with Woodrow Wilson. The people bought Harding's shiny package. President Harding's death in 1923 brought Vice President Calvin Coolidge into office. After completing Harding's term, Coolidge campaigned on his own in 1924. "Keep Cool and Keep Coolidge," urged the Republicans. So the people did.

In 1936 the Republicans tried vainly to win the Presidency back from Franklin Roosevelt by running Alf Landon and Frank Knox. They assured the nation it could get "off the rocks with Landon and Knox," but the voters didn't believe them. On the rocks or off, they overwhelmingly asked for more of Franklin Roosevelt.

Harold Ickes, FDR's Interior Secretary, was one of the deadliest phrasemakers ever to take aim at a political enemy. During the 1940 pre-convention period, someone asked Ickes if he had heard a speech by 38-year-old Tom Dewey, who wanted the Republican nomination. "No," said Ickes, "I did not listen because I have a baby of my own." Ickes took care of wealthy Republican candidate Wendell Willkie in the 1940 campaign by calling him "the barefoot boy from Wall Street." After that, Willkie's determination to be plain folks just didn't take. Ickes came through again in the 1948 race between President Truman and Thomas Dewey. Referring to Dewey's restrained manner of campaigning, Ickes spoke of the "elusive Dewey, the candidate in sneakers." This label did Dewey no good.

In the 1952 campaign, when the war in Korea was a primary issue, one of General Eisenhower's speech writers thought up a catchy, potent slogan. "I shall go to Korea," promised the candidate. A few cynics asked "What for?" But most people assumed that somehow Eisenhower's presence in Korea would end the war's bitter toll in blood and treasure.

In this same campaign of 1952 the Republicans blamed the Democrats for the war in Korea. That wasn't all. The Democrats were "soft" on communism said the Republicans, and besides had permitted corruption to thrive in government. Wrapping it all up in a pithy phrase, the Republicans labeled their opponents the party of "communism, corruption, Korea." The phrase cut deep and may well have helped Eisenhower's big victory.

Richard Nixon thought so well of the slogan, "I shall go to Korea," that he tried a similar one when he ran for President against John Kennedy in 1960. He would go to the Soviet satellites, he said, to assure the people in Russian bondage that their American friends hadn't forgotten them. Somehow, though, the retread didn't give the mileage of the original. Nixon lost the 1960 election and the nations under the Soviet yoke had no visit from our President-elect.

Slogans will always be part of the campaign apparatus. Among those that had moderate success were Theodore Roosevelt's Square Deal, Woodrow Wilson's New Freedom, Harry Truman's Fair Deal. In his 1960 speech of acceptance in Los Angeles, John F. Kennedy spoke of a New Frontier. This frontier, he explained "is not a set of promises—it is a set of challenges. It sums up not what I intend to offer to the American people, but what I intend to ask of them." The new phrase quickly caught hold. Only time could tell whether it would stick or pass into limbo like so many others.

In their pursuit of the Presidency, candidates make promises that they hope will bind voters to their cause. Sometimes, as in the 1960 presidential campaign, Democrat and Republican sound much alike. If party labels are removed it is difficult to tell which platform is which. No Republican candidate today opposes the great social changes that were written into law by Democrat Franklin Roosevelt's administrations, though many Republicans still regard FDR's Presidency as a disaster for the country.

Today's candidates offer different methods for achieving the party's goals, of course, but they're fairly close on the substance of big issues. Repeatedly in the 1960 campaign, Republican candidate Nixon declared that his objectives were similar to Democrat Kennedy's but that the Republicans had better ways of fulfilling them. Nobody was surprised that such statements by Mr. Nixon gave certain Republicans violent political indigestion. The party, of course, has a sizeable conservative, right wing. These Republicans found much of their 1960 platform hard to take.

As a campaign progresses, each candidate may borrow attractive items from his competitor. Both candidates in 1960 promised the country

> strong defense and security
> expanded programs of air, naval, military, and space research
> efforts at disarmament
> a new try to create world peace
> increased social security benefits
> higher minimum wages
> rehabilitation of blighted cities
> relief for high-unemployment areas
> expanded public housing
> medical care for the aged
> relief for the farmer
> federal help for education
> better enforcement of civil rights laws

In their zeal to win votes, candidates do all the things that may help. Kissing babies in public is a sure sign of a candidate's political intentions. The Kennedy family, both in 1960 and in earlier political battles, made much of "Coffee with Kennedy." At innumerable coffee sessions in the homes of family, friends, neighbors, and supporters, the Kennedys steadily pressed their cause. When John Kennedy couldn't appear personally, he could call on his "sisters and his cousins whom he reckons by the dozens—and his aunts."

During the 1960 campaign Kennedy rode a mule for the benefit of newspaper photographers. Nixon gave a speech to deaf mutes and thereby got good newspaper space. Sooner or later most candidates visit some American Indians and get photographed in Indian headdress. A classic in this line was Calvin Coolidge's widely published picture in the over-sized regalia of an Indian chief.

In the course of a campaign, the presidential aspirants use whatever special talent they can attract to their cause. Since the days of Franklin Roosevelt, actors seem to have been partial to the Democrats. In the 1960 campaign a flock of Hollywood celebrities came aboard the Kennedy band-wagon. In part, at least, this was to be explained by Kennedy family connections in Hollywood. The Republicans, not to be outdone, have also succeeded in marshaling a corps of lead-ing personalities from show business.

The party campaign managers think up ideas that will sting the opposition, and perhaps even deliver a one-two punch. During the 1948 Truman-Dewey contest, the nation was treated to a "Democratic Record Show." The Democrats included in the presentation a period of absolute silence. This was described by the announcer as Dewey's explanation of important questions of the day.

The Republicans came up with a "Truth Squad" in the 1952 campaign of Eisenhower and Stevenson. The Squad was supposed to trail the Democratic candidate for Presi-dent, listen to his speeches and then set the record straight on the spot. This meant that in effect the Republican Truth Squad went along on the Democratic candidate's tour. At many an airport the Truth Squad planes roared overhead while the Democratic candidate shouted his speech on the ground below. At every stop the Squad would set up micro-phones and answer the enemy's statements with the "truth." This was a tiring and difficult assignment for the Repub-licans and results could not easily be measured. The Truth Squad must have satisfied the Republican chieftains, though, because they also used it in 1956 and again in the 1960 campaign.

In every campaign there is heartbreak that often centers

around the word "If." If only the candidate had included
this state or that city in his tour. If only he had spoken up
here or kept quiet there. If only he had put more time on
this phase of the campaign instead of that. In short, if only
he had had the wisdom of hindsight when he decided where
to go, when to go, and what to say when he got there.

In the Hughes-Wilson campaign of 1916, Republican
candidate Hughes visited California. With Mr. Hughes were
some party leaders who were political enemies of the California Governor, Hiram Johnson. Johnson had a low opinion
of the Republican politicians attached to Hughes and
wondered why the candidate tolerated such company. At
one point, candidate Hughes and Governor Johnson were
in the same Long Beach Hotel. Hughes neglected to make
a courtesy call on the governor before leaving for Los
Angeles. This was a slight to a sensitive and important
political leader. Governor Johnson then and there washed
his hands of his party's presidential candidate. Without
Johnson's support Hughes lost the state and the presidential
election with it.

Another tragic "if" has already been discussed in connec-
tion with the Cleveland-Blaine contest of 1884. The Rever-
end Mr. Burchard's remark about "Rum, Romanism, and
Rebellion" cost Republican candidate Blaine enough votes to
tip New York into the Democratic column. With it went his
chance to become President.

President Eisenhower, shortly after his candidate, Nixon,
lost the 1960 election, discussed still another "if." About two
weeks before the election, Negro leader and minister Martin
Luther King had been arrested in Georgia after taking part
in a sit-in demonstration. A member of John Kennedy's
campaign staff suggested that the Senator telephone Mrs.
King to express his sympathy. The candidate promptly
called, offering to help her husband win his freedom. The
Senator's younger brother, Robert, then telephoned the
judge in the King case to ask that the minister be released.

To the Negroes and to supporters of civil rights, the phone calls meant that candidate Kennedy cared about this issue. At a rally in Atlanta, Dr. King's father rose to say he had intended to vote for Nixon but now he had changed his mind. "Jack Kennedy," he said, "has the moral courage to stand up for what he knows is right."

Senator Kennedy, said the elder Mr. King, "was willing to wipe the tears from my daughter's eyes. I've got a suitcase of votes and I'm going to take them to Mr. Kennedy and dump them in his lap."

These words were telegraphed to Negroes all over the nation. More than a million pamphlets describing the incident were distributed by the Kennedy organization. Under the title, " 'No Comment' Nixon Versus a Candidate With a Heart, Senator Kennedy," the Kennedy group got their message across.

On Sunday before election day the pamphlets were distributed in front of Negro churches throughout the country. It seems safe to say that Kennedy's narrow victories in Illinois, Michigan, and South Carolina were made possible in part, at least, because of heavy Negro support. If the Negro vote in these states had gone the other way, Mr. Nixon would have been elected President.

A poll by the public-opinion expert, Dr. George Gallup, showed that seven out of ten Negroes voted for the Democratic ticket. It is easy to believe that the Kennedy phone calls and the explanatory pamphlets helped produce this result.

After the election returns were in, a sad President Eisenhower remarked that "a couple of phone calls" had put the Negro vote into the Democratic column. This, he felt, was unfair. His own record as President, he believed, should have satisfied the Negroes that the Republican party was their true champion. Unhappy Republicans could only muse, "If only Nixon had made those phone calls . . ."

Post mortems may be a silly and futile exercise, but after

every election, especially the close ones, the diagnoses fill the air. As the examples prove, some presidential campaigns have been won by a few votes. An extra speech, an extra effort—even an extra phone call or two—can sometimes make the difference between victory and defeat. Speaking out on an issue, or maybe keeping quiet, can sometimes swing a city's vote. This in turn might decide the state vote. The electoral vote of a particular state might determine which man wins the Presidency. This is why the candidates run themselves ragged before election day. This is why they race from one public appearance to another and sometimes come back for a second, third, or fourth visit before the campaign closes. The candidates must assume that this city or that state must be won if victory is to be achieved.

The bulk of voters may, as some experts think, make up their minds even before the campaign starts. All the speeches, television shows, newspaper stories, and ballyhoo may make no difference to them. Their decision has been reached, often as a matter of party loyalty. Many Democrats stay Democrats through thick and thin; many Republicans are similarly dedicated. But the candidates dare not take even these sure voters for granted. Why? Because many of them may not care enough about a particular campaign to register or to vote.

It is a disappointing fact that between a third and a half of eligible voters throw away their voting rights because they are lazy or indifferent. Such "Democrats" and "Republicans" do their party's candidate no good. The candidates worry about this and try to stimulate this group enough to bring them out to the polls on election day.

There is also a sizeable group of "Don't Knows" or "Undecideds," voters who haven't made up their minds. They, too, are important because their strength is needed to put the winner over the top. So while each candidate wants to hold tight to his loyal supporters, he also wants to attract the independent or undecided voters. This explains much of the frenzy of the campaign.

Each side organizes special committees to welcome into its fold dissatisfied members of the opposition party. Franklin Roosevelt, whose name was often hissed by the business class, always had a "Businessmen's Committee" for FDR. A certain number of merchants, manufacturers, and financiers liked FDR and his ideas. They were willing to go to bat for him, politically, to give campaign funds, and to make speeches for him. On the other hand, a number of rich Democrats helped organize the "Liberty League" to fight FDR in the 1936 campaign.

The Republicans, in their effort to woo disillusioned Democrats, offer hospitality to any Democrats who can't stand their party's candidate. Republican candidates Herbert Hoover, Alf Landon, Wendell Willkie, Tom Dewey, Dwight Eisenhower, and Richard Nixon tried to win the support of Democrats opposed, respectively, to Franklin Roosevelt, Harry Truman, Adlai Stevenson, and John Kennedy. This is part of the game. Everybody expects to see these special committees blossom at election time when each party tries to entice voters from the rival candidate.

In the 1884 Cleveland-Blaine election, a group of Republicans deserted Blaine because, they said, he was "a candidate who is an unfit leader, shown by his own words and his acknowledged acts . . . to be unworthy of respect and confidence; who has traded upon his official trust for his pecuniary gain; a representative of men, methods, and conduct which the public conscience condemns and which illustrates the very evils which honest men would reform."

These Republicans, as could be expected, were ridiculed by the regular Republicans as "Mugwumps." What did this label mean? "Mugwumps," came the answer, means "Ishmaelites, Dependents, Soreheads, Pharisees, Goody-Goodies, or Assistant Democrats." Other Republicans had a one-word description of Republicans who voted Democratic: "Traitors."

In earlier decades, the tempo of the campaign was much slower than it is today. William McKinley in 1896, Warren G. Harding in 1920, and Calvin Coolidge in 1924 conducted "front porch" campaigns, remaining close to home or headquarters. They didn't feel it necessary to carry their political torch into every corner of the land. They left the day-by-day campaigning and vote-chasing to their managers and lieutenants. These men were professionals who knew their business well and produced victories, even though the candidates themselves were relatively inactive.

Candidates are sometimes unaware of the guerilla tactics that victories are made of. When Republican Benjamin Harrison won the election of 1888, the party chairman, Matthew Quay, congratulated him. "Providence," said President-elect Harrison, "has given us the victory." Telling this to a friend later, Quay added, "Providence hadn't a damn thing to do with it."

Many a campaign starts in low gear. The candidate and his managers try to give it momentum, to build public interest. They strain to get crowds that will steadily grow bigger and more enthusiastic. This is hard to achieve. If the candidate is colorless, if the campaign issues lack excitement, or if there are big competing diversions—World Series baseball, freakish weather, national or international crises—public interest may focus elsewhere. Party leaders may then have to beat their drums louder.

No candidate can afford to be ignored. Every appearance —at an airport, whistle stop, rally, parade, or public dinner —must be well-attended. The crowds must be brought out, at almost any cost. Nobody has ever done this more skillfully than John F. Kennedy in 1960. His managers saw to it that wherever he landed, wherever he stopped, there was a respectable, if not overflowing crowd to receive him.

The Republican "Truth Squad," when asked about the

size of the crowds turning out for Kennedy, replied with scorn, "Schoolchildren." It's true that Mr. Kennedy talked to pupils in school during the primary fight, when adult audiences weren't always easy to find. This didn't make him too unhappy, though. He knew that when the pupils went home, they talked to their parents. The fact remains that, schoolchildren or not, a candidate doesn't look like a winner unless he pulls a crowd. If he can't attract adults, he's usually glad to settle for students.

In whipping up support for a presidential candidate, the managers keep in steady touch with the small, local leaders who have direct contact with the voters in their district. A local politician may have varied reasons for supporting the presidential candidate. He may do it out of loyalty or affection or the bonds of tradition. He may do it because his own reputation as a political leader is at stake. He may do it because he expects big things to happen if his man comes in —recognition by the White House, jobs for local political supporters, an "in" with the right people in Washington. Or he may be involved in a local election. By nuzzling up to a popular presidential candidate, the local politician may pick up a bonus of votes that would not ordinarily be there.

Some presidential candidates, while personally popular, have not been able to lend their appeal to candidates for lesser office. Dwight Eisenhower could not transfer the magic of his name to the Republican candidates who ran for Congress during his Presidency. Three out of four congressional elections went Democratic during that time.

But Franklin Roosevelt did a lot of good to aspiring Democrats who stuck close. Hyman Shorenstein, a minor Brooklyn politician, once explained it all to a worried supporter who was running for local office. "Did you ever go down to the slip," asked Hymie, "and watch the ferryboat from Staten Island come in? You ever watch it, and look down in the water at all those chewing-gum wrappers, and the banana peels and the garbage? When the ferryboat comes into the wharf, automatically it pulls all the garbage in, too. Well, stop worrying. Franklin D. Roosevelt is your ferry-boat."

Campaign managers use standard tactics to make a presidential candidate look good. They try to time his appearance in town with the lunch hour. This gives him a natural crowd. Before he arrives the party leaders have passed the word— or the orders—that all the faithful are to be on hand. Bus-loads from out of the district are commonly brought in to beef up the local partisans. Candidates frequently appear at factory gates during noontime or at day's end, when the workers pour out. In some communities children are released from school to see and hear the candidates. Every body helps.

The managers want news photos and stories, and radio-television reports to show big, excited crowds flocking to the candidate. This in itself is worth a lot of votes. Some people will simply go along with a winner—any winner. A candidate who regularly draws poor crowds may be written off by some voters as a sure loser. The candidate makes the most of the crowd's size—and then some. He tries to get into his speech such comments as "big crowd," "great turnout," "huge and warm reception." Listeners and readers far from the scene are expected to take notice.

One test of a candidate's strength, of course, is the reception he gets in "hostile" territory. The Republican candidate who pulls a big audience in a poor, working-class neighborhood; the Democratic candidate who draws well in a high-class or "silk-stocking" district, has won a headline. Each side makes political capital out of any such victories.

To some extent the candidate adjusts his speech to the audience he is addressing. A trade-union audience gets one talk, a convention of business executives another, a farm audience still a different one. A meeting of clubwomen, a gathering on a college campus, a meeting of city precinct workers, a rally in New England and another in Mississippi would not get the same oration. Yet in these days of electronically-fast reporting, a candidate has to choose his words with care. He mustn't promise to one group what he has just denied to another. He mustn't have one set of principles for one audience and a different set for another. What he says in Los Angeles is instantly known in New York. To switch policies according to the climate or the region or the nature of the audience is today full of political peril. His enemies, in and out of the party, will quickly expose him if he resorts to doubletalk.

The fact is that most candidates stick fairly close to a basic set of ideas. Some stick so close, in fact, that they try the nerves of the reporters who go along on the campaign train. Newspapermen who accompanied vice presidential candidate Lodge in his 1960 tour, groaned when he began to deliver "The Speech." They knew it as well as he. But Mr. Lodge was talking to different voters all the time. He was satisfied with "The Speech," and his primary purpose was not to keep reporters happy, but to impress the citizens with the qualifications of the Nixon-Lodge team. "The Speech," he felt, did just this.

Each candidate makes his appeal as broad as he possibly can. Within each campaign organization are many separate divisions, each intended to lure a particular group of voters. Usually these include:

new voters
unregistered citizens
nationality groups
foreign born
religious groups
youth
Negroes
aged
liberals
businessmen

    organized labor
    voters grouped in professions and occupations
    independent, unaffiliated citizens
    voters from the other party

The candidate goes after each of these groups with specially prepared bait—letters, pamphlets, speeches, posters, billboards, newspaper stories and advertising, rallies, entertainment, and other forms of propaganda. In pursuing the Negro vote, for example, the candidate will draw on Negro celebrities from the show world, sports, and politics to strengthen his appeal. His aim is to convince the Negroes that their future lies with him and his party.

Party managers usually create special "citizen" or "volunteer" groups in presidential campaigns. These are composed, presumably, of men and women who are not ordinarily engaged in politics, but who think enough of the candidate to offer their time and labor in his cause. Many of these volunteers temporarily overcome their distaste for politics because the candidate appeals to them. Such groups help the candidate look popular, with support that ranges far beyond his party.

Sometimes the Citizens or Volunteers come into conflict with the regular party workers. Relations between the two groups can get to be very bad. The regulars tend to look down on the Citizens and Volunteers as impractical reformers, do-gooders, and amateurs. These, in turn, may think the regulars are political hacks, professional politicians whose chief principle is, What's in it for me? When conflict between the two groups threatens, the party high command must enforce peace. Only then can the candidate hope to harvest all possible votes. It may become a complicated task to make a truce between such hostile groups but it has been done many times. At the end of the campaign the combatants have sometimes resumed their warfare.

Much is heard about public opinion polls in the presidential election. Do they correctly record public opinion? Do they influence public opinion? Do they create public opinion? How much confidence can be placed in them?

While the polls have occasionally been discredited, they remain a familiar part of the presidential campaign. Long before the nominating conventions, the polls tell us who the popular favorites are. At regular intervals the public is informed of the changing odds on the various contenders in the two parties.

After the nominating conventions have made their choice, the polls test public opinion on the candidates' chances for election. Naturally a candidate who is leading thinks well of this kind of measure. To him it is a valuable device for testing public opinion in a democracy. If the poll shows he's trailing, he will probably ridicule it as unreliable and misleading.

The polls have suffered a few disasters in presidential campaigns. One occurred in 1936 when the magazine *Literary Digest* predicted that Alf Landon would defeat Franklin Roosevelt in a landslide. As the history books tell, the opposite happened. Landon carried the electoral votes of two states—Maine and Vermont. The other forty-six went for FDR for a second term.

How did the *Literary Digest* come up with its unfortunate prediction? The magazine polled names in telephone books and auto registration lists. Nobody on the publication staff figured that in the sick economy of 1936, lots of Americans had neither telephones nor automobiles. Most folks who enjoyed these conveniences were strong for Landon. That left a big majority for Franklin Roosevelt. In his first term, FDR had satisfied the poor, the unemployed, and the hopeless that he was trying to give them a New Deal. Until someone better came along they would stick with FDR.

So while the *Literary Digest* built up a big majority for Alf Landon, the voters did the opposite. By its miscalculation the magazine suffered a fatal blow to its prestige. It folded after the election.

Later opinion-takers refined and improved the methods used in sampling public feeling, as explained in Chapter 2. The polls were generally accepted up to the 1948 Truman-Dewey contest. In that election the pollsters, and most everybody else, predicted that Dewey would win. But in a classic upset, Harry Truman defeated Thomas Dewey. Truman had narrowly won enough in key states to snatch their electoral votes and thereby to win the election. An unforgettable picture right after the election was a grinning Harry Truman, holding aloft the front page of the *Chicago Tribune* which read, "Dewey Defeats Truman." The pollsters, the predictors, the newspaper writers—and most citizens—saw the impossible happen. A man of whom everybody said "Not a chance" squeaked through to become President of the United States.

Mr. Truman, understandably, had a low opinion of the polls and he didn't shrink from saying so. He knew all along, he insisted, that he would win. The polls, he said, were worthless. Both parties have nevertheless continued to study poll results carefully. Candidates frequently ask public-opinion polling organizations to conduct private tests on their own chances of election or of popular feeling on some issue. This tells the candidate how the wind blows. Candidates sometimes tailor their speeches accordingly. This is delicate business that is done on a private, confidential basis. No candidate wants this information to leak out. He can't have it said that he is just a follower, that he finds out what it's safe to say before he says it. Though the polls will continue to be attacked and defended, nobody doubts that they are here to stay.

The whole business of presidential campaigning obviously costs a lot of money. Where does it all come from? How is it spent? What happens if expenses exceed income?

Financing is one of the biggest headaches of party managers. Nobody really knows how much it costs to elect a President of the United States, but experts who have studied the subject have some pretty good clues. The 1956 presidential campaigns of Eisenhower and Stevenson were estimated to cost around $17,000,000. This figure was offered as a minimum, conservative sum.

The 1960 Kennedy-Nixon campaign came a good deal higher. An estimate by the respected research organization, the Brookings Institution of Washington, was $26,000,000. But this figure included only expenditures by national committees. It did not take account of additional millions spent by state and local committees for the presidential candidates.

Why does nobody know the true figures? Because the raising and spending of campaign money is too complicated and too circuitous for anybody to follow: partly this complexity is unintentional, partly it is by design. If the law about campaign expenditures were strictly followed, a candidate would have to run a very limited operation. His personal appearances, his television and radio programs, his posters, billboards, buttons, and advertising would shrink to a fraction of what we have come to expect in a presidential campaign.

The American people want to see and hear their candidate for President, or so the candidates believe. In any case, the candidates in recent years have tried hard to get their message to the voters—all of them—wherever they might be. This takes money, lots of it. And the costs go up year by year. A half-hour of national television time cost $60,000 in the 1956 campaign, but $78,000 in the battle of 1960. The candidates rely more and more on this dollar-devouring technique. They are convinced that television gives them the best coverage. Future candidates are likely to use it more, not less.

Some scholars and experts have suggested that the government should pay the whole cost of presidential campaigning. This way, they feel, the competing candidates would be fairly matched. Neither would have the advantage of unlimited money; neither could conduct a "saturation" campaign. It would become impossible to buy an election with a flood of campaign money. Some authorities go further. The primaries, they say, should also be government-financed and government-supervised. Only then would the rich and the poor aspirant stand an equal chance.

It is common for presidential candidates or their partisans to accuse each other of trying to buy their way into the White House. Sometimes the evidence supports the accusations. An investigation by the United States Senate showed that spending in the 1920 pre-convention Republican fight reached record sums. Expenditures on behalf of General Leonard Wood went above one and three-quarter million dollars, and exceeded $400,000 for his chief rival, Governor Frank Lowden. Neither man won the Republican nomination, partly, at least, because of the belief that they were tainted by money.

In the 1960 contest, a top Republican strategist charged that John Kennedy had spent $7,000,000 to win the Democratic presidential nomination, not the $250,000 that Kennedy officially listed. Kennedy's victory at the Los Angeles convention, said this Republican, "proved the American dream that any boy can hope to grow up to win the Democratic nomination for President, providing his father has $400,000,-000. I guess it is now only $393,000,000."

Brookings Institution experts say that John Kennedy's run for the Democratic nomination cost over $900,000. They call this figure a minimum, though, because it does not include money spent for Mr. Kennedy by local and state supporters.

After ten months in office, President Kennedy showed his worry about the problem by appointing a committee to study it. Campaign funds, said the President, have always been supplied "by private contributions, with the candidates forced to depend in the main on large sums from a relatively small number of contributors. It is not healthy for the democratic process, or for ethical standards in our government, to keep our national candidates in this condition of dependence. I have long thought that we must either provide a federal share in campaign costs, or reduce the cost of campaign services, or both."

Neither party has been enthusiastic about having the government assume full financial responsibility for the campaigns. Both parties seem to feel they can do better by the present system, though it is complicated, inefficient, and unpredictable. The Republicans are less willing to change than the Democrats. Over the years the Republicans have had access to more rich supporters than the Democrats.

Nevertheless there are laws on the subject, but they are so loosely written that they don't cramp any finance manager's style. Legally the national committee is limited to an expenditure of $3,000,000 in a presidential campaign. But there is no limit to the number of committees that may go to work for a candidate. Each may legally spend its own $3,000,000.

According to law a person may contribute a maximum of $5000 to a national campaign. Corporations are prohibited from making any contributions and so are trade unions. The intention of the law, of course, was to prevent wealthy corporations and well-to-do unions from buying the election for their favorite candidate.

So much for the law's intention. What about the practice? Actually a corporation president may contribute as an individual up to $5000. So may every member of his family. So may every member of his board of directors and each family member. So may every vice president and all members of his family.

Though a labor union may not contribute, it may create a "political action" committee that can give freely. Such committees are busily involved in all presidential contests.

Would-be givers may also contribute to local and state committees. These, in turn, may funnel the receipts into the national presidential war chest. This is within the law.

Why do people give? Some give out of conviction. Certain donors believe that only the Republican party can be safely entrusted with the destiny of our nation. They may regard Democrats as unsound financially, as emotionally soft-headed, and as generally unfit to run the country. Contributors to the Republican campaign may also have a big financial stake in Republican policies. These donors will favor a party that, historically, has been more attentive to the needs, the problems, and the profits of businessmen.

Democratic contributors, on the other hand, may feel that their party has done a better job of running the country. They think it is more attuned to meet the crises that have bedeviled the nation and the world over the years. Or they may feel that they are better served financially by Democratic policies. Their particular business or line of work may have prospered under Democratic administrations. The line between self-interest and sentiment sometimes gets very faint.

Some contributors give without any particular emotion. A man might give because he expects something in return, possibly some legislation that will benefit him financially. Or it might be that he or his wife is looking hopefully for some job. This might be something as Olympian as a Cabinet post, or an ambassadorship, or heading up a big federal department. There is a long tradition in both parties of awarding ambassadorial plums—Paris, London, Rome—to big campaign contributors. Recently this practice has been cut down. More and more it has been realized that such jobs call for more than just wealth and generosity. Career diplomats and talented people from private life have been moved into various embassies that formerly were awarded to wealthy givers. Up to the present time, however, some choice embassies have continued to be reserved for big contributors.

Donors understand, generally, that a gift to the party carries no guarantee, nor even promise, of anything. The money is given in the hope that with victory will come a reward. Yet many men are willing to write substantial checks to the party and take their chances. Some men give to both parties as a form of insurance. Their gifts, they hope, will keep them in good standing no matter who wins. Some hope for nothing more than the opportunity to get a favorable reception at the White House on some occasion.

Throughout political history, the parties have depended on just a few contributors for the bulk of their money. The Republicans, it has been explained, have an easier time of it, because they have more wealthy supporters to call on. In recent years, though, the trend has been for more campaign money to come from modest givers, and less from the big donors, the "fat cats." Both parties conduct energetic drives for contributions from people who may give $1, $5, $10, or $100. The parties go after these small sums because, obviously, the total yield is sizeable. There's another important reason, too. The party managers feel that a citizen who makes a contribution, however small, becomes a worker. He has enrolled, so to speak, and committed himself to the party. He can be counted. Probably he will influence others to do the same.

Aside from the big donations and the little ones, how does the party get its money? A favorite device is the money-raising meal. From time to time the party runs a dinner or luncheon or breakfast that may produce a good yield of dollars. The Republican Lincoln Day dinners, the Democratic Jefferson-Jackson Day dinners are the best known. Party workers, usually in upper-bracket jobs, and well-to-do citizens are willing or obliged to pay $25 or $50 or $100 or more to sit down and break bread together. At these events the political party in power has an advantage, because it can produce as chief attraction the President of the United States himself. A new adaptation of this device is the closed-circuit television dinner. The party faithful in different parts of the country are privileged to see and hear the President, who may be speaking from a dinner in Washington.

Many special celebrations are also held, both in and out of campaign season. As an election nears, a hot candidate becomes a strong attraction. His appearance at a dinner will draw a heavy turnout at a fancy price. Substantial contributions, over and above the price of admission, may also be expected. During the 1960 campaign John Kennedy even pulled two hundred guests to a $1000 a plate luncheon. Because of the pressure of legislative business in Washington, Senator Kennedy could not even attend. He made good a few days later at a breakfast and the well-heeled guests went away satisfied.

Not every candidate can attract the financial angels. When President Truman ran for a full term in 1948, nobody gave him a chance. Few Democratic millionaires came forward to pick up the bill for the campaign. From day to day there was doubt whether the campaign would go forward at all because the money just wasn't there. The presidential campaign train itself got stalled in the West for lack of funds. An anguished appeal brought enough money to get the train on the rails again. President Truman resumed the whistlestop campaign that shortly produced a victory over his well-financed rival, Thomas Dewey.

Much of the time the national committees are in the red. As a presidential campaign ends, a committee may be in alarming financial trouble. At the close of the 1960 campaign, the Democratic party had a deficit of a whopping three and three-quarter million dollars. This was the greatest debt ever amassed by a political party. In every campaign the national committees groan publicly about their deficit as they appear to be going under. But there seem always to be enough good men who are ready to come to the aid of their party. No matter how dark the financial prospects, a call for help usually gets an answer. The party angels, the party faithful, and the political jobholders dredge up the needed funds. A new round of dinners and fund-raising activities gets under way and the red ink gives way to black.

As long ago as the log-cabin-and-hard-cider campaign of 1840, the politicians sensed the advantages in razzle-dazzle campaigning, of injecting excitement, drama and some hokum into the campaign. They borrowed a bit from vaudeville and circus in putting their show together. In the 1960's many of the same tactics are used. They are more varied, more sophisticated—and infinitely more expensive.

And this is the stuff of victory. Work, worry, money, in amounts that can't be measured by common-sense standards. Only a man who is willing to pay this price has a chance for the Big Prize. A man who is able to pay this price can probably handle the Presidency.

CHAPTER SEVEN

WHO ELECTS
THE PRESIDENT?

MOST AMERICANS, IF ASKED "WHO ELECTS THE PRESIDENT?"
would answer firmly, "The people, of course." The fact is
that the people do not elect the President. Not directly,
anyway.

The men who wrote the Constitution back in 1787 did
consider letting the people themselves vote for President,
but they decided against it. They had strong reasons that
we'll examine in just a moment.

But if the people were not to elect the President, who
should? The Congress? The state governors? These and other
possibilities were examined by the Founding Fathers—the
men who wrote the Constitution. They grappled with the
problem all through the summer of 1787. Finally they came
up with an answer by creating a special group of electors—
the Electoral College—who would actually vote for the
President.

Debate about the Electoral College has continued off
and on through most of our history. At election time, every
four years, the argument is sure to grow hot. When the

election excitement dies down, the wrangling about the Electoral College subsides, too.

Why do many people—plain citizens, politicians, political scientists, and scholars—object to the Electoral College? Why do other plain citizens, politicians, and experts defend it? Why has it survived these many years almost untouched, though many Americans are against it? What suggestions have been made for changing it? Why are the prospects for change poor? Why, in other words, are we stuck with our method of electing a President, when there's so much opposition to it?

To understand why the Founding Fathers set up the Electoral College, we must re-create the atmosphere of the times. Present at the Constitutional Convention in 1787 were men from the following twelve states:

> Delaware
> Pennsylvania
> New Jersey
> Georgia
> Connecticut
> Massachusetts
> Maryland
> South Carolina
> New Hampshire
> Virginia
> New York
> North Carolina

Rhode Island, the thirteenth state, sent no representatives.

The delegates, some from big states and others from little ones, eyed each other with some suspicion. Virginia, New York, Pennsylvania, and Massachusetts had large populations. They wanted power that corresponded to their size. They demanded that representation in Congress be based on the number of people in each state. But the states with small populations, such as New Jersey and Delaware, insisted that all states have equal representation in Congress. They feared that they would be swallowed up if representation were based on population. Here were the makings of bitter disagreement—and this, of course, is what happened.

Each delegate wanted all possible advantages and no disadvantages. Nobody wanted to go home with a Constitution that discriminated against his own state. Yet each wanted to go home with a Constitution. Every delegate, that is, wanted the Constitutional Convention to succeed. Everybody understood the need for unity, for forging a single strong nation that could stand against time. Every delegate knew that compromise was necessary, that neither big nor little states could have their way on every issue.

Certain feelings ran through many of the Convention delegates. These feelings determined the kind of Constitution the men wrote. They all knew, for example, that the country needed a strong executive. But they did not want him so strong that he might wield tyrannical power. They favored an independent national legislature, too. But they did not want the lawmakers to dwarf the executive. They wanted a system of courts that could judge the laws impartially, but not dominate the rest of government. As we know, the delegates adjusted their differences and came up with a nicely balanced scheme of separate executive, legislative, and judicial branches. Each branch was strong, but no branch could overwhelm the others.

Another general feeling at the Constitutional Convention was that the common people must be kept in their place, politically. In spite of the ringing words of the Declaration of Independence, the Founding Fathers favored only a limited amount of democracy. They did not believe that the ordinary citizen could handle political power. He would not know what to do with it, they feared. He might, for example, use it against the people who had won riches, property, and social standing. He might try to overturn society altogether and bring down the very men who held places of leadership in the new republic.

There was a fairly common feeling in colonial times that ability, intelligence, and riches ran together. A man who had acquired wealth, it was assumed, was brainy and therefore able to vote wisely. A poor man was a doubtful risk. He probably was lacking in judgment, or sobriety, or intelligence. Otherwise he would have made good in the competitive economic world.

Few delegates at the Convention had confidence in the ability of everyday citizens to elect a President. The plain people were believed to be ignorant and provincial. They would probably favor a local personality for President, instead of seeking the outstanding man in the country. Why give such people the vote?

While these ideas may seem aristocratic and old-fashioned, lots of people believed them in the days when our Constitution was written.

Another point. The Founding Fathers had the task of creating "a sovereign nation of many sovereign states," a federal system. This means a government in which each state, though it is part of the United States of America, continues to be highly independent and important. A federal system calls for a delicate balance between the national government and the individual states. The finished product had to be a nation that was strong and united, and could win the respect of a skeptical or hostile world. But the separate parts—the states—had to retain their identity and individuality, and much power besides. The small states, especially, were sensitive about this. They were determined to protect their sovereign position in the nation and their equality with the big states.

The Founding Fathers worked out some ingenious compromises to solve these problems. They created a powerful central government but at the same time reserved many rights for the individual states. The struggle between large and small states was resolved by setting up a unique Congress of two parts. In the House of Representatives, it is population that counts. Representation is based on the number of people living in the state. Every state, no matter how thinly populated, has at least one member in the House of Representatives. But in the United States Senate, every state, no matter how small its population, has two senators. Alaska, with 200,000 people has the same number of United States Senators as New York, with a population of sixteen million. By this plan the large states have an advantage in the House of Representatives; the small states get theirs in the Senate.

We come back now to the question of electing the President. The small states, in weighing the idea of a direct vote of the people for President, asked, What does this plan do to our standing as one of the sovereign United States? They felt that direct election by the people—one citizen, one vote—would put them at a disadvantage. Their importance would be overshadowed by the big, populous states. So the small states spoke a firm No to this proposition.

What were the alternatives?

Somebody suggested that Congress would be the right group to name the President. This was objectionable, too. If the power to elect a President rested in Congress, the balance between legislative, executive, and judicial would be upset. A President created by Congress would probably be subservient to it. To win election he might seek the favor of congressmen. If he wanted to be re-elected, he would be further inclined to try to please them. The Founding Fathers wanted the President to be eligible for re-election, but they did not want him to depend on the votes of congressmen—for election or for re-election. Letting Congress elect the President would not bring forth the sort of able, independent leader the Fathers had in mind. So this idea was dropped, too.

What about having the state governors make the choice? Here again, this might give too much influence to state leaders. It would disturb the relationship between states and central government that the Constitution makers sought. The Chief Executive of the nation must not become the creature of the state governors.

To sum it up, the Founding Fathers decided that voting for President was too important a responsibility to be left to the people. They could not let Congress do it, nor could they give it to the state governors. Was there any other possibility? Through a painful evolution of proposal and counter-proposal, the writers of the Constitution finally reached a solution—the Electoral College.

The first thing to know about the name "Electoral College" is that the word "college" refers only to a group of people who have a certain duty to perform—to cast ballots for President and Vice President of the United States. The "college" has no building or campus or headquarters. The electors from the various states do not get together as a group in the nation's capital or anywhere else. The electors of each separate state do meet in their own state capital to vote for President on a specified day. The Constitution says that each state legislature shall decide how to pick its electors.

How many electors is each state entitled to? As many as its total representation in Congress. Each state, no matter how small its population, has at least one member in the House of Representatives, plus two in the Senate. Every state, therefore, has at least three electors. A heavily populated state has a big electoral group, equal to all its members in the House of Representatives plus its two senators. But every state, no matter how small in population, has a minimum of three electors.

In 1960 there were 437 members in the House of Representatives and 100 in the Senate. The sum of these two numbers, 537, was the exact number of electors in the nation in that year. And this was the actual number of votes cast for President.

The Constitution says that a majority of electoral votes

is needed for election. A bare majority of 537 is 269. This is the magic number that candidates John F. Kennedy and Richard M. Nixon pursued in their hard-driving campaign through the summer and fall of 1960. By the Twenty-third Amendment, ratified in 1961, the District of Columbia won the right to vote in presidential elections. Three electoral votes were allotted to the District.

What kind of men would the electors be? How would they be chosen? This was left to the state legislatures. But the Founding Fathers expected that outstanding citizens, experienced in national affairs, would be named. The electors, it was hoped, would be leaders in their states. Officeholders in the United States government, including members of Congress, were barred from serving as electors. The idea was to get independent men who were not involved in the national government. It was hoped that these men would neither use improper influence nor be subject to it.

The Constitution originally said that the electors should vote for two qualified men. The one who achieved a majority of all the electoral votes would become President. The man with the next highest vote would become Vice President. By the Twelfth Amendment the electors were required to vote separately for President and Vice President.

The Founding Fathers wanted to be sure that the electors scanned the whole country in their search for a President, that they didn't just settle for local persons of limited ability. Therefore the electors were told by the Constitution that of the two men they vote for, at least one must come from outside their own state.

The writers of the Constitution did not foresee the rise of political parties in the United States. They expected the electors to choose a President from the country as a whole. But when George Washington announced in 1796 that he would not accept a third term, political parties began to appear. These parties, acting through their leaders in Congress and elsewhere, decided whom they wanted for Presi-

THE FEDERAL ADMINISTRATIVE ORGANIZATION

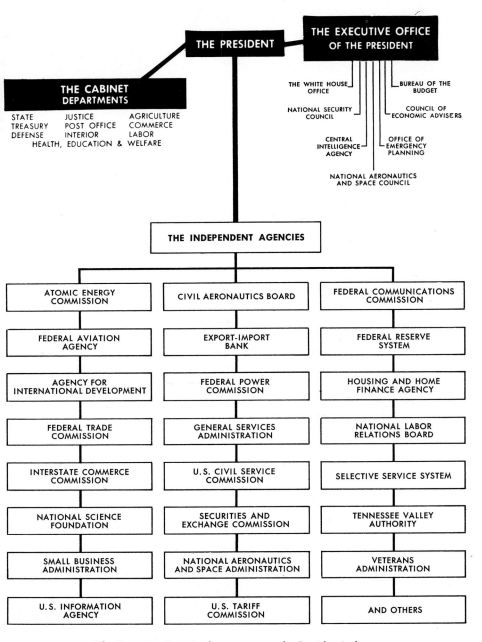

THE PRESIDENT

THE EXECUTIVE OFFICE OF THE PRESIDENT

THE WHITE HOUSE OFFICE

BUREAU OF THE BUDGET

NATIONAL SECURITY COUNCIL

COUNCIL OF ECONOMIC ADVISERS

CENTRAL INTELLIGENCE AGENCY

OFFICE OF EMERGENCY PLANNING

NATIONAL AERONAUTICS AND SPACE COUNCIL

THE CABINET DEPARTMENTS

STATE   JUSTICE   AGRICULTURE
TREASURY   POST OFFICE   COMMERCE
DEFENSE   INTERIOR   LABOR
      HEALTH, EDUCATION & WELFARE

THE INDEPENDENT AGENCIES

ATOMIC ENERGY COMMISSION	CIVIL AERONAUTICS BOARD	FEDERAL COMMUNICATIONS COMMISSION
FEDERAL AVIATION AGENCY	EXPORT-IMPORT BANK	FEDERAL RESERVE SYSTEM
AGENCY FOR INTERNATIONAL DEVELOPMENT	FEDERAL POWER COMMISSION	HOUSING AND HOME FINANCE AGENCY
FEDERAL TRADE COMMISSION	GENERAL SERVICES ADMINISTRATION	NATIONAL LABOR RELATIONS BOARD
INTERSTATE COMMERCE COMMISSION	U.S. CIVIL SERVICE COMMISSION	SELECTIVE SERVICE SYSTEM
NATIONAL SCIENCE FOUNDATION	SECURITIES AND EXCHANGE COMMISSION	TENNESSEE VALLEY AUTHORITY
SMALL BUSINESS ADMINISTRATION	NATIONAL AERONAUTICS AND SPACE ADMINISTRATION	VETERANS ADMINISTRATION
U.S. INFORMATION AGENCY	U.S. TARIFF COMMISSION	AND OTHERS

The Executive Branch of government—the President's direct
responsibilities and the organization of his department.

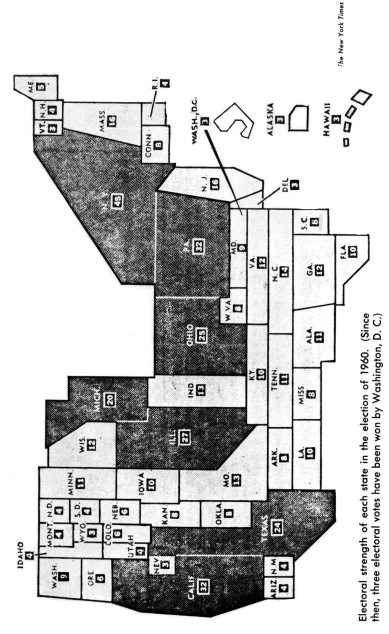

Electoral strength of each state in the election of 1960. (Since then, three electoral votes have been won by Washington, D. C.)

The total number of electoral votes is 537, so the majority required to win is 269. The seven largest states, shown in dark shading on the map, have 205 votes. Of these the three largest states — New York, Pennsylvania and California—have 109. Electoral votes are shown in boxes on each state, and the area of each is distorted in proportion to the number of its votes.

Herblock in The Washington Post

"By golly, if I had a part in this campaign . . ."

Politics in a democracy calls for more than talk.

HOW MANY OF US VOTED?

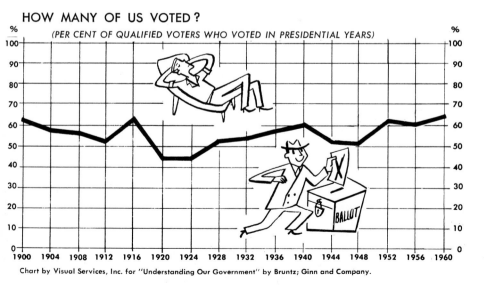

(PER CENT OF QUALIFIED VOTERS WHO VOTED IN PRESIDENTIAL YEARS)

Chart by Visual Services, Inc. for "Understanding Our Government" by Bruntz; Ginn and Company.

Getting out the vote is a major problem in a democracy.

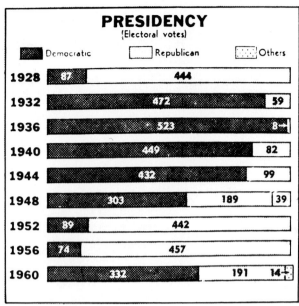

PRESIDENCY
(Electoral votes)

	Democratic	Republican	Others
1928	87	444	
1932	472		59
1936	523		8
1940	449	82	
1944	432	99	
1948	303	189	39
1952	89	442	
1956	74	457	
1960	332	191	14½

Electoral battles from 1928 to 1960 showing the strength of the parties.

The New York Times

THE GERRY-MANDER.

The original gerrymander. Odd-shaped electoral districts in Massachusetts, approved by Governor Elbridge Gerry in 1812, are embellished by the artist to create a new species of political animal.

Courtesy of The Bettmann Archive

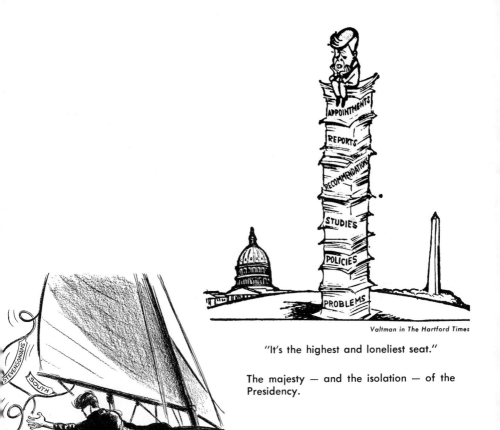

Valtman in The Hartford Times

"It's the highest and loneliest seat."

The majesty — and the isolation — of the Presidency.

Mauldin in The St. Louis Post-Dispatch

"Loose ends."
Candidate Kennedy has some rough sailing after winning the Democratic nomination, 1960.

Aldor in El Tiempo, Bogota

"Inauguration."
The incoming and outgoing Presidents contemplate their future at inauguration, 1960.

Crockett in *The Washington Star*

"And I didn't mean all I said about you."

After the election—cold comfort.

"Jack and the beanstalk."

Promises flourish during a campaign.

Seibel in *The Richmond Times-Dispatch*

"On Guard!"
Before the TV debates, 1960.

Long in *The Minneapolis Tribune*

Victorious candidate Truman enjoys the early edition of the Chicago *Tribune* that jumped to the wrong conclusion, November 4, 1948.

FDR tosses out the first ball — an ancient presidential rite.

White in The Akron Beacon-Journal

Republican and Democrat interpret the
same statistics in the 1960 election.

Crook in Newsday, Garden City, L. I.

"Chained to the past."
A Democratic view of candidate Nixon, 1960.

York in The Louisville Times

"The trend went that-away."
Party managers give their own interpreta-
tion to poll results in the 1960 campaign.

"They laughed when I sat down at the piano."

Lyndon Johnson plays a Dixie melody. A tribute to the vice-presidential candidate's campaign success in the South, 1960.

"Do you think we can get it through without taking it apart?"

Campaign platforms often come apart in the halls of Congress.

"The Hon. Member of the Forty-Fourth Congress"

An oft-heard complaint — Congress talks too much.

"Hope springs eternal."
Candidate Nixon fishes for Democratic votes, 1960.

"Go ahead! The chair is pre-heated for you."

The hottest seat belongs to the President. Eisenhower leaves and Kennedy enters upon office, 1961.

"I just kept piling them up,
and before I knew it . . ."
Criticism of Kennedy's campaign promises, 1960.

Vicky in The New Statesman, London

"Anything you can do, I can do better . . ."

Party platforms tend to resemble each other.

"Long Abraham Lincoln a little longer."
After Lincoln won re-election in 1864.

Harper's Weekly, November 26, 1864

"Prestige"

An American presidential election may strike foreigners as disruptive or violent. After the election, they are puzzled to watch the political parties close ranks and to see a united nation roll up its sleeves and get back to work.

Keppler in Puck

"The Crown Prince"

President Theodore Roosevelt names William Howard Taft as his successor, 1908.

"March 4, 1869
    A giant among the pigmies."

"March 4, 1870—
    A pigmy among the giants."

General Grant shrank in public esteem shortly after he became President.

Tom Dewey, in search of the 1948 Republican nomination, is initiated into the Oregon Cavemen Club after a dinner of raw meat.

President Calvin Coolidge becomes Chief Leading Eagle of the Sioux tribe, 1927.

War Department, Washington, April 20, 1865.

$100,000 REWARD!

THE MURDERER

Of our late beloved President, Abraham Lincoln,

IS STILL AT LARGE.

$50,000 REWARD

Will be paid by this Department for his apprehension, in addition to any reward offered by Municipal Authorities or State Executives.

$25,000 REWARD

Will be paid for the apprehension of JOHN H. SURRAT, one of Booth's Accomplices.

$25,000 REWARD

Will be paid for the apprehension of David C. Harold, another of Booth's accomplices.

LIBERAL REWARDS will be paid for any information that shall conduce to the arrest of either of the above-named criminals, or their accomplices.

All persons harboring or secreting the said persons, or either of them, or aiding or assisting their concealment or escape, will be treated as accomplices in the murder of the President and the attempted assassination of the Secretary of State, and shall be subject to trial before a Military Commission and the punishment of DEATH.

Let the stain of innocent blood be removed from the land by the arrest and punishment of the murderers.

All good citizens are exhorted to aid public justice on this occasion. Every man should consider his own conscience charged with this solemn duty, and rest neither night nor day until it be accomplished.

EDWIN M. STANTON, Secretary of War.

DESCRIPTIONS.—BOOTH is Five Feet 7 or 8 inches high, slender build, high forehead, black hair, black eyes, and wore a heavy black moustache, which there is some reason to believe has been shaved off.

JOHN H. SURRAT is about 5 feet, 9 inches. Hair rather thin and dark; eyes rather light; no beard. Would weigh 145 or 150 pounds. Complexion rather pale and clear, with color in his cheeks. Wore light clothes of fine quality. Shoulders square: cheek bones rather prominent; chin narrow; ears projecting at the top; forehead rather low and square, but broad. Parts his hair on the right side; neck rather long. His lips are firmly set. A slim man.

DAVID C. HAROLD is five feet six inches high, hair dark, eyes dark, eyebrows rather heavy, full face, nose short, hand short and fleshy, feet small, instep high, round bodied, naturally quick and active, slightly closes his eyes when looking at a person.

NOTICE.—In addition to the above, State and other authorities have offered rewards amounting to almost one hundred thousand dollars, making an aggregate of about TWO HUNDRED THOUSAND DOLLARS.

Photo Courtesy National Park Service

A reward is posted for the murderer of President Abraham Lincoln, 1865.

Courtesy of the New York Historical Society, New York City

"Jackson is to be President and you will be HANGED."
Andrew Jackson's enemies called him a hangman and assassin in the election of 1828.

Candidate Horace Greeley accepts baby kissing as part of campaigning, 1872.

Becker in Leslie's Illustrated News. Courtesy of The New York Historical Society, New York City

The Democratic view of the Whig candidate, General Zachary Taylor, 1848.

Ballyhoo in the "Log cabin and hard cider" campaign for Harrison and Tyler, 1840.

BUNKER-HILL
Convention.

THE FARMER OF NORTH BEND.

ALL Delegates to the Convention, who may choose to enter Boston by the way of Cambridge, are invited to meet at the

TOWN HALL IN CAMBRIDGE-PORT,

on the morning of the 10th of Sept., and join in the procession which will there be formed at **8 O'CLOCK,** *precisely,* and proceed to Boston under escort of the "**CAMBRIDGE TIPPECANOE CLUB,**" accompanied by the Boston Brass Band.

The "*Concord Tippecanoe Club,*" will join in the procession with the **GREAT BALL!**

It is expected that a large number of delegates will assemble as above, on horseback, and unite in the procession until they reach Boston, when they will join the main cavalcade.

Delegates will find accommodations for their horses and carriages in Cambridge-port, and Delegates from a distance, who may arrive on the 9th, will be furnished with accommodations by applying at the Town Hall.

☞ *A prompt attendance is earnestly requested.*

Per order of the Cambridge Committee of Arrangements,

ISAAC LIVERMORE, Chairman.

Cambridge, September 3, 1840.

Caleb Rand, Printer, Charlestown Square.

dent. Private party meetings in Congress—caucuses—were usually called for this purpose.

Once the political parties began to put forward their own candidates, the responsibility of the electors shrank. They no longer had to search for suitable nominees. All they had to do was vote for the choice of their own party.

Beginning in the 1830's, national nominating conventions were called by the chief political parties. At these meetings, held every four years right up to the present day, the parties name their candidates for President and Vice President. The electors merely approve the selection of the nominating convention.

When and how do the electors do their duty? On presidential election day, the Tuesday after the first Monday in November, the people go to the polls and vote for either Democratic or Republican electors. When the people vote for Democratic electors, they feel they are voting for the candidate named by the Democratic party. Similarly, Republicans pull the lever for Republican electors, because they expect these electors to vote for the Republican party choice.

Over the years, the states adopted the policy that the electors winning the greatest number of votes carry the state. This means that the electors who get more votes than their opponents, are in. They do not need a majority of all the votes. They simply require more than any other group of electors. Nor does it matter that they might have won by just a few votes. So long as they surpass their rivals, they have won. Such a state, we say, has "gone Republican" or "gone Democratic." The votes received by the losing party win no electors and therefore do not count.

It has not always been this way. There was a time when voting was done by districts in each state. The electoral vote might then be divided, with some districts going Republican and others Democratic. But gradually all states adopted the "general ticket" plan. This means that the state's entire electoral vote goes one way or the other.

To sum up, then, the popular vote elects electors in each state. The electors in turn elect as President and Vice President the men nominated by their national party conventions.

The importance of the electors is obviously less than the Founding Fathers intended it to be. In many states the electors' names do not even appear on the ballot. Once they are selected by their state party organizations, their names are filed in the state capital. On the presidential ballot it merely says, "Electors for . . ." and the names of the party candidates for President and Vice President are printed in.

To win the Presidency, a candidate needs a majority of all the electoral votes in the nation. This is known, usually, hours after the polls close on election day. Strictly speaking, of course, it is only the electors who are elected on this day. But the nation accepts the idea that if Republican electors win, they will naturally cast their ballots for the Republican candidate. If Democratic electors win, everybody expects them to vote for the man named by the Democratic nominating convention.

The electors go through their voting exercise the following month, on the Monday after the second Wednesday in December. Meeting in the fifty state capitals and, starting in 1964 in the District of Columbia as well, they cast their ballots for President and Vice President. The results, but not the electors, are sent to the national capital. There on January 6, two weeks before inauguration, the ballots from all the states are counted, as the combined Senate and House of Representatives look on. The Vice President of the United States, who is the president of the Senate, is in charge of counting the electors' ballots and announcing the results. In January, 1961, this presiding officer was Vice President Richard M. Nixon. It was his ironic duty to announce to the world the election of his campaign rival, John F. Kennedy.

The Constitution says that if no candidate receives a majority of electoral votes, the decision shall then be made by the House of Representatives. When this happens, each state casts one vote only. A majority of all the votes is necessary for a choice. The members of the House of Representatives pick from among the three candidates with the highest number of electoral votes. The Senate has the job of picking a Vice President from the two candidates with the largest number of votes.

In the election of 1800, two candidates for President—Thomas Jefferson and Aaron Burr—received an equal number of electoral votes. The electors who supported Jefferson and Burr wanted Jefferson to become President, of course, and Burr Vice President. But the result of their voting was nevertheless a tie. Therefore, in accordance with the rule laid down in the Constitution, the election was taken to the House of Representatives. There Jefferson was chosen President. To prevent a repetition of a tie vote, the Twelfth Amendment, ratified in 1804, said that the electors should vote separately for President and for Vice President.

In 1824 again, no candidate received a majority of electoral votes. So the House of Representatives, choosing from among Andrew Jackson, John Adams, and William Crawford, elected Adams.

Our electoral system makes it possible for victory to turn on just a few votes. A candidate may win the popular vote in a state by a narrow margin. Even though he barely squeaks through, he gets the state's entire electoral vote. Once he has a majority of electors in the nation, he's in. In some states he may lose by large popular majorities. At the final tally, his opponent may have more popular votes than he, but the candidate with a majority of electoral votes does not worry what the popular vote shows. In the 1960 election, John F. Kennedy became the fourteenth President to poll less than a majority of popular votes. He had won in the electoral college, but his popular vote was less than a majority of all the votes cast.

This electoral system has been under attack for many

years. More than a hundred times, efforts have been made in Congress to change the electoral machinery. Up to the present none has succeeded. Seasoned observers of presidential politics feel that none is likely to succeed.

Let's examine the complaints, see what improvements are offered, and find out why the reformers have had such unhappy results.

The present electoral system has repeatedly been called unfair and undemocratic. Critics say that it results in the waste of large numbers of votes. If a state goes for a candidate by even a small number of votes, he wins the entire electoral vote of that state. His opponent, who may have polled almost as many votes, gets no electors to his credit. His popular vote, according to this theory, has been thrown away. Across the nation, the loser may have been nosed out in state after state. All his popular votes count for nothing.

Some people are troubled by the fact that a candidate, to win the whole electoral vote of a state, does not even need a majority of popular votes. A plurality is enough. This means that he need only get more popular votes than the other candidates, even though this is less than a majority. Let's say, for example, that in a presidential election a million votes are cast in a certain state. The Republican candidate, we'll say, gets 400,000 votes. The Democratic candidate gets 300,000 votes and three candidates of minor parties get 100,000 votes each. The Republican candidate wins the entire electoral vote of the state with his 400,000 popular votes. This is a plurality—more votes than anybody else— though it is not a majority. A candidate, in other words, may capture a state's electoral vote with less than a majority of popular votes. A plurality can give him victory.

It is even possible for a candidate to win the Presidency, though his opponent has amassed more popular votes. In 1888 Benjamin Harrison won a majority of electoral votes but Grover Cleveland received 100,000 more popular votes. How can this happen? A candidate may win by a few votes in several states and thereby pick up enough electoral votes to win the Presidency. His opponent may win in other states by big majorities and actually top the winner in total popular votes in the nation. But remember, it is electoral votes that count. The Constitution says so in clear language.

Another complaint about the present system is that the final electoral count may be misleading. The winning candidate may appear to have swamped his opponent. This is because winner takes all, even in a state where he wins by a handful of votes. The electoral count does not show how close the candidates might really have been. It is often a surprise, after reading of an electoral landslide, to discover that in popular votes the candidates were fairly close. In the election of 1896, for example, Republican candidate William McKinley won 271 electoral votes against William Jennings Bryan's 176. But in popular votes, McKinley received a little more than 7,000,000 and Bryan received around 6,500,000. In the 1940 election, Franklin Roosevelt won 449 electoral votes against Willkie's 82. But in popular votes, Mr. Roosevelt had 27,000,000 against Willkie's 22,000,000.

Still another objection to the Electoral College plan is the fact that electors, in spite of tradition and general expectation, are not required by the Constitution to support their party's choice for President. In fact the Constitution says nothing about political parties. It simply confers on the electors the responsibility of electing a President and Vice President.

It has already been explained that the Founding Fathers assumed that the electors would be an elite group—leading citizens who would be familiar with national affairs and with national personalities. These electors, it was hoped, would search the land for "continental characters," men of towering ability and quality. From such men the electors would pick two—one to be President, the other Vice President.

The rise of political parties and the national nominating conventions changed all this. Now the party conventions do the picking. The electors, chosen by popular votes in all the states, merely rubber-stamp the party choices.

In some states, electors are "pledged" to vote for the persons named by the party. But pledged or not, the electors are expected by the voters to go along with the party. Electors are nevertheless free to exercise their Constitutional privilege and vote their personal choice rather than the party choice. Some electors have done this.

In the 1960 contest, electors in several states ran unpledged. This means they reserved the right to ignore their party's selection. In Democratic Mississippi and Alabama the voters elected a total of fourteen electors who spurned the Democratic party nominee, John F. Kennedy. The electors hoped to use their voting power to force a change in the Democratic civil rights program, which they felt was obnoxious. They thought they might dicker with the rival presidential candidates and give their electoral support to the one who offered them the best deal.

The uncommitted electors from the South had another idea, too. There was a chance that neither major candidate would win a majority of electoral votes. In that case the election would go into the House of Representatives. Here each state, regardless of size, would cast one vote. A group of southern states might hold the balance of power here. They could then throw the Presidency to the candidate who was most receptive to their ideas on civil rights.

Twice, in 1800 and 1824, the President has actually been chosen in the House of Representatives. It could happen again. Some experts are worried about this because when the House elects a President, every state delegation, irrespective of size, casts a single vote. Alaska, for example, would cast one vote. New York, with seventy-four times more people, would also have one vote. This disturbs some experts as sadly undemocratic.

Students of government are also unhappy that the present

electoral system tends to freeze power in certain states. The Democratic party in Vermont and the Republican party in Georgia have always been small and have fought against hopeless odds. Under the all-or-nothing plan by which electors are elected, these minority parties stand little chance of capturing their states' electors. Everybody knows in advance which electors will win. In spite of this long-standing condition, cracks sometimes appear in the solid Democratic South and in the rock-ribbed Republican states of New England. Believers in democracy hope to see more vigorous party competition in the states that have for many years been safe for one party. This process may be helped by the great mobility of the American people—with Republicans invading Democratic territory and vice versa.

What remedies have been offered to cure the ills of the electoral system? One is that the President should be elected by a straight popular vote and the Electoral College abolished. The candidate with the most votes would become President. This appears logical and democratic. But there are strong objections to it.

If the candidate with the most votes won the Presidency, and the Electoral College were eliminated, our whole federal system would be shaken and perhaps damaged. At the present time the electoral vote of each separate state is a recognized part of the election process. If this were done away with, the importance of each state in electing the President would be reduced. Such a change could have the effect of erasing state lines. The small states, of course, would lose most influence. Under the present system, even the smallest state has three electors—equal to its member in the House of Representatives and its two members in the Senate. Relatively, then, a small state would lose power if a straight popular vote were substituted.

This plan would also encourage the formation of additional parties, which would have a better chance of success on a

one-for-one vote than they do now. By collecting their individual votes from all over the country, these parties would
show up better and offer a stronger challenge to the major
parties. This could undermine the two-party system and
foster a multi-party system in its place. The two-party idea
is deeply rooted in American political life. The general feeling seems to be that it has worked out well in the United
States. How would the people feel about a mushrooming of
"third" parties? This could become a real problem if we
changed to a straight popular vote. Splinter parties would
be encouraged because every vote they won would count.

Another point. What if the popular vote were very close?
Would the results be accepted as readily as they are now?
Some experts think not. Under present conditions, a candidate takes the state's entire electoral vote or nothing. Across
the nation, the electoral vote of each state tumbles as a unit
into one column or the other. The candidate with a majority
wins the Presidency. But suppose there were no electoral
vote and the popular results in the nation were close, very
close. Would the losers accept the result, as they do now?
Or would they question it, demand a recount, start legal
action, and try to tip the scales enough to change defeat into
victory? Some authorities believe that an advantage of the
present electoral system is its definiteness and its finality.
This, they feel, might be lost in a straight popular vote.

Another plan for reforming presidential elections is the
"district system." Its aim is to eliminate the "winner-take-all"
policy. Each state would be divided into districts that are
roughly equal to congressional election districts. Each district would elect an elector by majority vote. The voters of
a state would also elect two electors at large, to correspond
to the state's two United States Senators. Some districts might
go Democratic, some Republican; the majority in each district would decide.

Let's see how this might work. Assume that a particular

district is Republican. It would elect a Republican elector even though the state as a whole were Democratic. At the present time the Democratic majority in such a state would win the state's entire electoral vote. Under the district plan, every district would reflect the choice of its own majority. A district would not lose out because most voters in the state favored the other party.

This idea appeals to many citizens as more fair and democratic than the present all-or-nothing system. The district plan, however, has flaws that spoil its chances for success. The chief opponents of this plan are voters who are generally called "liberals." This group, whose strength is concentrated in the cities, can usually be expected to support certain kinds of legislation. These include minimum wage laws, protection of labor unions, public housing, unemployment insurance and other forms of social security, government medical care, aid to education, and strong civil rights laws. Why should liberal voters oppose the district system of electing electors? Because they believe it would work to the advantage of conservative voters, many of whom live on farms, in villages, and in suburbs. These non-city people have usually had little sympathy for liberal ideas, and have tried to block them or hold them to a minimum.

The liberals are afraid of any plan that makes districts the basis for electing electors. Liberals are convinced, for example, that many congressional districts have purposely been shaped to include a majority of Republican, rural, and conservative voters, and only a minority of liberals. This tactic of patching together a voting district to assure victory to one political party is called "gerrymandering" in honor of Elbridge Gerry of Massachusetts. He is credited with having developed the system back in 1812, as governor of his state. He approved the creation of a strange-looking voting district that would give his party a safe majority. Because the district looked like a salamander, someone said it should really be called a "gerrymander." This name stuck. The idea—molding election districts to benefit the party in power—took root and is practiced by both parties on occasion.

The result of gerrymandering is that there are many odd-shaped districts that contain Republican or conservative majorities. These election districts send legislators to Congress who tend to favor the Republican point of view. Generally these lawmakers use their power to write conservative laws and oppose liberal ideas. Conservatives usually dominate in state legislatures, too, partly because of the way districts are set up. Liberals therefore oppose any scheme of presidential voting that would permit conservative-minded districts to acquire power.

Under the present electoral system a candidate for President knows that he must appeal to the masses of city voters if he is to carry their state. The rural sections in many states are less important, numerically, than the big population centers. The parties, therefore, build their platforms with one eye on city dwellers. They must do this to attract the liberal, big-city vote. This is true of both Democrats and Republicans.

Remember that closest to the heart of most politicians, even closer than party principles, is the need to win. Without victory there are no jobs, no base of operations, and no magnet to draw party workers and contributions. Party principles are frequently stretched to fit the needs and the wishes of the voters. The Republican party, as an example, has long accepted the social security program. But back in the days of Franklin Roosevelt, when these laws were proposed, the Republicans had no use for them. Reading the popular pulse, however, the Republicans sensed that they had no choice.

Every politician knows that the big-city vote is a necessary ingredient of success in a presidential election. New York, Philadelphia, Chicago, Detroit, Boston, Los Angeles, San Francisco, Dallas—with their millions of votes—are key points in every presidential contest. ⸆The party and the candidate fight hard for this vote. Proof of this may be seen in the party platforms, in the candidates' speeches, and in the campaign circuit they follow.

Suppose, however, the candidate did not have to appeal to the city vote. Suppose he had to swing only districts that the conservatives controlled. Would he be as liberal as he is now forced to be?

According to some authorities, the electoral college system propels the parties and the candidates in the direction of liberalism. A candidate, by rolling up a big majority in the cities, may ensure victory, no matter how the rest of the state votes. Liberals, generally speaking, know that they have an armory of power in the millions of big-city voters. They realize, also, that they have most to lose by any change that would reduce the power of the urban vote.

After the 1960 election a prominent Republican leader said, "We lost the 1960 election because we lost the Negro vote. The Republican party must concentrate all its efforts to win the Negroes back to the Republican party." How could this be done? Only by liberalizing the Republican platform, by making it more attractive to Negro voters. The Negro bloc, like the city bloc of voters, is a prize to capture.

This does not mean that the Republicans will outdo the Democrats in liberal promises. It does make clear that some Republicans are alert to the need for expanding the ranks of their party. These Republicans may be expected to exert pressure at platform-writing time to get a more liberal platform, one that will lure Negroes into the Republican ranks.

Experts in presidential politics have pointed out that the rural, conservative, and Republican groups have an advantage in the selection of state legislators and Congressmen because of the way election districts are now drawn. Liberal groups, on the other hand, with their big-city support have an advantage in the choice of a President. The rural and suburban vote gives strength to the conservatives;

the sheer numbers in the big cities strengthen the liberals.

This, according to some authorities, makes a fairly good balance. To change the electoral system to a district plan would mean that the liberal, city folks would lose their chief center of influence in government—the Presidency.

Whenever a change in the electoral system is proposed, the opposition springs to action. The trade unions, whose strength is chiefly concentrated in cities, know that the present system is advantageous to them. Many others share their feelings—Negroes, the foreign-born and their families, religious minority groups, lower-income workers, many Democrats. The spokesmen for all these groups oppose a change to a district plan of electing electors. This means that such a change has a slim chance for success.

Another suggestion for altering the electoral system is a plan of proportional representation. By this method each party would get a proportion of the electoral vote equal to its popular vote in each state. A party that polled 45 per cent of the popular votes in a state would get 45 per cent of the electoral vote. A party that won 55 per cent of the popular vote would get that percentage of the electoral vote. Under the present system, of course, the first group would get no electoral votes. The other, with 55 per cent of the popular vote, would get the entire electoral vote.

On the face of it, the proportional system sounds fair and desirable, but it would never be accepted by the liberals, for reasons already mentioned. They are against any change that might weaken their influence. Under proportional representation the liberals would lose their advantage in the large population centers. Here they frequently pile up enough votes to swing the whole state. Under a proportional plan, though, their power would be cut. They would get only that portion of the electors that their popular vote entitled them to. The rural and conservative voters would win the rest.

Another objection to the proportional plan is that it would

encourage third parties, sometimes called "minor" or "splinter" parties. Under the present plan, a small party knows its chance of winning a state's electoral vote is nil, because all electoral votes go to the party that shows up best in the popular vote. Under proportional representation, though, a small party would actually get as many electors as its popular vote justified. In the nation as a whole, it might pick up a substantial number of electors. This would spur the small parties to work harder. We might then see the growth of numerous splinter parties that could threaten the two-party system.

Most voters understand that under the two-party system a presidential candidate, in order to win, must make a broad appeal. He can not be just the candidate of the rich, or the poor, or the businessmen, or organized labor, or the farmers, or the bankers, or of East, North, South or West. He must offer a program and a personality that are reasonably acceptable to voters of different economic, geographic, and political backgrounds. He must, in short, be a man who can look and act like a President of all the people.

He may, of course, lean this way or that. He may arouse the enthusiasm of one group or another. But he can not be their exclusive property. He can not campaign on a platform that promises to exalt one group and destroy another. Not if he expects to win.

The result is that the American President, under our two-party system, has been both tolerant and tolerable. He may be ardently favored by one party, but the other party must be able to live with him.

Individuals, of course, may exercise their right to believe a particular President is intolerable. When Franklin Roosevelt became President, at least one wealthy opponent decided that the United States was no longer a fit place to live. He departed for Europe until the Roosevelt regime would end.

The American President is a great moderator, a great pacifier, a leader of all Americans, no matter how they live or how they think. This is an accepted and approved feature of our two-party system. It would be endangered by the growth of small parties. Leaders of third parties usually are men with a mission, men with a limited popular appeal, men who usually advocate strong political medicine. The American people have had no experience with this kind of President. There is no evidence that they want to start.

Let's consider a few more suggestions for changing the electoral system. One is to continue the all-or-nothing part of the present system, but to abolish the Electoral College itself. How would this work? The party winning most of the popular votes would still get the whole electoral vote of the state, but the electors would not actually meet in their state capital to cast ballots for President and Vice President. The electoral votes won by each candidate would simply be totaled, and the one with a majority of electoral votes in the nation would become President.

This plan would prevent an elector from ignoring his party's choice and voting for somebody else. In 1960 this threat made the election uncertain right down to the day the electors actually cast their ballots. Under the proposed change, the President would be elected as soon as the tally of electors was completed. There would be no opportunity for electors to bargain with candidates while holding the nation in suspense.

While many people like this idea, it has one danger. Suppose, after the electoral votes were counted, and the President chosen, he should die? There would be no meeting of the electors in the state capitals to make another choice, because there would really be no electors under this plan. This shows that the role of electors, though greatly contracted since the days of the Founding Fathers, may still be important. In certain circumstances the responsibility of electors can be very great.

Coupled with this proposal for doing away with the Electoral College is a suggestion that whoever wins the most electoral votes becomes President. The winner would not require a majority of electoral votes, as at present. He would simply need more than his competitors. This might be a plurality of the electoral votes, rather than a majority. Whoever topped the list of candidates, even if he did not have a majority, would be the victor. By this plan, the need to decide an election in the House of Representatives would disappear. The possibility of candidates and congressmen bargaining over the Presidency would end.

The small states could hardly be expected to rejoice about this proposal. They are satisfied with the present plan: if no candidate gets a majority of electoral votes the decision goes to the House of Representatives. When this happens, each state casts one ballot, however small the state might be. The small states do not intend to surrender this reservoir of prestige and power.

We have now examined the leading suggestions for changing our system of electing a President. We can see that for every proposal there is opposition—strong opposition. No group is willing to make a change at its own expense. It would rather continue with the present set-up, though admitting its defects.

Some experts, while they acknowledge faults in our electoral system, say that the alternatives may be worse. Their argument is that no system can be satisfactory to everybody and that the evils of our present one are less serious than those in any proposal that has come forward. They add, also, that the defects of our accustomed method are obvious, but any new system may reveal faults that are not now suspected. These authorities caution against trading known troubles for unknown.

Remember that a change in the electoral system is possible only by amendment to the Constitution. This means that two-thirds of both houses of Congress must agree to the change. It then goes before the states. Three-quarters of them must approve it before it passes. This makes it relatively easy to block an amendment to the Constitution. With powerful groups opposed to each of the proposed changes in the electoral system, it is not likely that this system will be altered.

Every four years, at election time, much complaint will be aired about our antiquated system. Bills to change the Electoral College will overflow the congressional hoppers. They will be argued and fought over, as they have more than a hundred times already. But the system, from every available sign, will go on just the same.

CHAPTER EIGHT

MR. PRESIDENT

When the push of a button may mean obliteration of countless humans, the President of the United States must be forever on guard against any inclination on his part to impetuosity, to arrogance, to headlong action, to expediency, to facile maneuvers, even to popularity of an action as opposed to the rightness of an action. . . .

The nakedness of the battlefield, when the soldier is all alone in the smoke and the clamor and the terror of war, is comparable to the loneliness—at times—of the Presidency, when one man must conscientiously, deliberately, prayerfully scrutinize every argument, every proposal, every prediction, every alternative, every probable outcome of his action, and then—all alone—make his decision.

These eloquent words, spoken by Dwight Eisenhower at the close of his Presidency, sum up the majesty and the isolation of the biggest job in any free country of the world.

Harry Truman expressed it differently when, on April 12, 1945, he succeeded to the Presidency on the sudden death of Franklin Roosevelt. Talking to reporters the next day, President Truman said, "I don't know whether you fellows ever had a load of hay fall on you, but when they told me yesterday what had happened, I felt like the moon, the stars, and all the planets had fallen on me." Every President, from George Washington to John F. Kennedy, has felt this burden from the day he was sworn in to the day he left office.

George Washington, whose duties were light compared to those of a President in the 1960's, complained out loud of the work that bore down on him. He did not have time, said Washington, to think, to reflect, to read, to take a long and leisurely look at his job and at his country.

John F. Kennedy, after a few months in office, was asked by an old friend how he liked being President. "Well," said President Kennedy, "it is the kind of office that if you lost it, you shouldn't complain." At another time, harassed by the problems that are dumped on the President's desk every day, Mr. Kennedy mused, "Nixon should have won the election."

Some Presidents, of course, have enjoyed their work more than others. Among the ones who got a charge out of being President were Andrew Jackson, Theodore Roosevelt, who called it "bully," and Franklin Roosevelt. Other Presidents have had less enthusiasm for a job heavily weighted with burdens and toil. Among this group were John Adams, James Buchanan, Warren Harding, Herbert Hoover, and Dwight Eisenhower.

One thing is certain. The office grows steadily more complex and more punishing. The duties that are now imposed on the Chief Executive make the early Presidencies seem pleasant, if not restful. This may mean that in the future the unwilling, or reluctant candidate will probably not get very far. It is likely that a true draft of an undeclared candidate will not occur again, that only aggressive, eager candidates will stand a chance. The American voters, as they sense the demands made on the modern Presidency, will probably agree that it calls for a tough-fibered man who really wants the job; that the shy type could not survive its rigors.

The title "Mr. President" is a modest one for an office of

such great importance. Selecting the title was not easy. Some members of Congress, who in 1789 made the decision, favored "His Excellency." A committee of Senators felt that this was not grand enough for the size of the office. They proposed "His Highness, the President of the United States of America and Protector of Their Liberties." George Washington is said to have favored this one. But it and other titles with a regal and imperial flavor were turned down as inappropriate in a democracy. The various members of Congress then settled on "Mr. President." It seemed to be about right for a nation that had changed from an empire colony under a king into a republic in which the people were sovereign.

The Constitution says briefly what the President's duties are.

> He is commander-in-chief of the Army and Navy
> He may grant reprieves and pardons
> He makes treaties with the advice and consent of the Senate
> He appoints ambassadors, judges, and other officers with the Senate's approval
> He reports to Congress on the "state of the Union" and recommends laws that he feels are necessary
> He takes care that "the laws be faithfully executed"

This is an unimposing list of duties that gives only a faint clue of how the President spends his days—and nights. And there is no doubt that the Presidency is a day and night job.

The fact is that the duties laid on the President by the Constitution are only a meagre framework, so simple-sounding as to be misleading. As the American nation has grown in size and power, the people's expectations have grown, too. They have come to assume that the United States will be first in everything. They think it quite natural that this country should set a standard for the world in

> prosperity
> military strength

industry
education
individual and national well-being
scientific, industrial, and military research
invention
moral leadership
humanitarian responsibility

American citizens assume, also, that leadership in fulfilling these expectations will come from the White House.

If a distant nation falls under communist control, the American people think of it as a failure in our President. When another country achieves a great scientific break-through—say Russia's Sputnik in 1957 or the man-in-space in 1961—our eyes turn questioningly toward our own President. How did this happen? we ask. Why wasn't the United States first with the best, as usual? The American President feels called upon to explain, and to start immediately to close the gap that has been exposed.

As the range of presidential duties grows steadily greater, the Chief Executive must depend on assistants to help him do his job. Chief among them is the Cabinet. Authority to create this body comes from a line in the Constitution that says the President "may require the opinion, in writing, of the principal officer in each of the executive departments." These "principal officers," or Cabinet, have important executive duties, but the full responsibility for running the country remains with the President. If his helpers—in or out of the Cabinet—should bungle the job, the blame is laid on the President just the same. He is expected to repair the damage and to face the music if things don't come out right. A painful example was the 1961 fiasco in Fidel Castro's Cuba, where an invasion backed by the United States was smashed. The nation looked only to the President for an explanation.

Back in 1929 when the American economy went crashing, the people held President Hoover responsible, though he had scarcely started as Chief Executive. In the 1932 election the dissatisfied voters turned him out of office.

The Constitution says nothing about the way in which the President shall operate. It assigns him certain duties and time has added many more, but like every important executive, he is free to conduct his office as he sees fit. He may consult anyone he chooses and refer to the history books to learn how other Presidents acted. But when all his consultations and studies are over, the President—alone—must decide what to do. Rarely does it happen that two crises are alike. No matter how well he knows his country's history, no matter how familiar he may be with the Constitution and the nation's laws, the President can turn to no guidebook that prescribes the right course. He still has the awesome responsibility of making the decision. If he decides correctly, the nation and posterity will acclaim him. If the decision brings unhappy results, the history books will never forgive him. Abraham Lincoln, reflecting one time on the exposed, isolated position of the President, said:

> If I were to try to read, much less answer, all the attacks made on me, this shop might as well be closed for any other business. I do the very best I know how—the very best I can; and I mean to keep doing so until the end. If the end brings me out all right, what is said against me won't amount to anything. If the end brings me out wrong, ten angels swearing I was right would make no difference.

This quality of responsibility is part of every high administrative job, and especially of the Presidency. The burden is entirely and exclusively the Chief Executive's. It is indivisible. The people neither know nor care who helped him reach a decision. If it turns out badly, he and he alone will be held responsible.

Presidential style varies. Some Presidents have taken their cue from that line in the Constitution that says "he shall take care that the laws be faithfully executed." According to this

view the initiative belongs to Congress. The legislators decide
what laws the country needs. The President's mandate is
only to see that these laws are carried out. This is discussed
further in the next chapter.

In recent years, as national and international problems
have multiplied, this "passive" Presidency has given way to
a more active one. The pace of events has made this inevitable. No President could just sit it out these days as
chief custodian of the Constitution and the laws passed by
Congress. He would soon be engulfed—and so would the
nation—by the surge of events around him. But even active
Presidents work in different ways. This is clearly evident in
the Presidencies of Dwight Eisenhower and John F. Kennedy.

General Eisenhower succeeded to the Presidency after a
renowned career in the army. He had had slight experience
in civilian affairs and no interest in politics. To Mr. Eisenhower, politicians were an unfamiliar species and not very
attractive. Their ways of operating—the give and take, the
deals, the palavering, the time-eating, the stalling—were outside his experience and not to his taste. By training and
inclination he favored a crisp, efficient way of doing things
—with lines of authority clearly marked out. He wanted to
make his decisions and have them carried out with a minimum of confusion or delay.

When Mr. Eisenhower became President he organized his
many helpers in and around the White House in the manner
of an experienced general. Except for their civilian titles, the
men and women in the Executive Office of the President
might have been serving in a military organization. At the
top stood the President—as he must by law. Then came a
couple of confidential assistants and the Cabinet, who saw
the President frequently. Below them were many important
officials, but Mr. Eisenhower had only limited contact with
this group. Many of them prepared important material for
him, but he saw little of it. Their recommendations came to

him eventually, for approval and signature. He had little part, however, in the arguing, the thrashing-out of ideas that must precede any important decision. Mr. Eisenhower preferred not to listen to debate and controversy. He wanted the debaters to have had it out long before the issue came to him in final form.

Mr. Eisenhower liked his information in a tidy package. He preferred reading Westerns to the bulky, fact-heavy reports that came his way. Even the newspapers had little appeal for him. He wanted data only after it had been screened by a small group of trusted advisers. He wanted his presidential assistant to bring it in with a recommendation to approve or not to approve.

As President, Mr. Eisenhower met regularly with his Cabinet, who in his eyes were a general staff. He would throw out for discussion problems on which he wanted their help. He listened carefully and was strongly influenced by their attitudes. Frequently he shaped his decision according to the trend of Cabinet thinking. The phrase "chairman of the board" was sometimes applied to Mr. Eisenhower. It suggests that he consulted his Cabinet and honored their collective judgment in the way a leader in industry would respect the advice of his top trustees or board of directors.

In contrast to this "chairman of the board" approach is the method of President John F. Kennedy. His experience and personality were altogether different from General Eisenhower's and so was his style.

Mr. Kennedy was born into a political family. Both his grandfathers had come up the hard way, starting in ward politics in old Boston. Politicians of all sizes and shapes had walked through John F. Kennedy's life from infancy. He knew their way and loved it. He did not see politicians as people to be tolerated and then disposed of as quickly as decently possible. He welcomed and enjoyed their company, their talk, their schemes. Because he was one of the boys, he played their game—with brilliant success. Nevertheless, as Mr. Kennedy climbed the political ladder—member of the House of Representatives, United States Senator, and finally President—the character of his companions changed, too. He sought more intellectual and less political company, though he never lost touch with the practical, grass-roots politicians.

As President, Mr. Kennedy simply had to get involved not only with his official advisers but with lots of others in lower positions, too. His personality made this inevitable. He wanted to be in on all possible discussion. He wanted, personally, to study the raw material out of which decisions are made. He did his own reading, his own questioning, and a great deal of his own research. A President who felt this way was not likely to lean heavily on a Cabinet for advice. Mr. Kennedy summoned his Cabinet irregularly, rather than on a fixed, frequent schedule. He met with them as often as he felt necessary, just as he consulted many other people— individually or in groups, depending on circumstances. To some writers this appeared to be an untidy arrangement and a poor use of the collective ability of the Cabinet. Other observers felt the President should continue to feel free to call on anybody and everybody at will, even though the Cabinet as a whole might appear to be slighted.

Nobody can say which way is better. Many Presidents in the past have used outside, unofficial advisers. Sometimes Presidents have called on personal friends to do specific jobs, to serve as "trouble-shooters." Some Presidents have regularly passed over Cabinet officials, to call on lower-echelon staff for help. Back in Andrew Jackson's administration, his unofficial "kitchen cabinet" came in for much criticism, though there was nothing illegal about it. Woodrow Wilson used a friend, Colonel House, as his eyes and ears. Franklin D. Roosevelt trusted Harry Hopkins, an official below Cabinet status, with urgent presidential responsibility. In the early stages of his first Presidency, FDR was surrounded by a "Brain Trust," who helped, unofficially, to shape the President's New Deal.

No President called on as wide a range of helpers as President John Kennedy. He consulted people of all rank and of no rank in seeking advice. This practice inspired press stories that the President was confusing and even demoralizing his regular staff—Cabinet officers and others. Mr. Kennedy was accused of undermining the authority of high officeholders by assigning their responsibilities to special individuals and special groups. These were often called "task forces" which meant, usually, that they had a specific job to do for the President, after which they were dismissed. The harshest complaint was that President Kennedy was getting too much advice. Some newspapers charged that the President was surrounded by a flock of advisers—brilliant men, but with conflicting points of view. As a result, said the critics, Mr. Kennedy was irresolute and indecisive when the times called for the very opposite.

Friends of Mr. Kennedy justified his policy by claiming that it made for a more "creative" approach to problems. They conceded that it lacked orderliness and precision. They argued that the benefits to the President and to the country outweighed the faults.

One thing is clear. Mr. Eisenhower's clean-lined procedures would have been unacceptable to Mr. Kennedy. And Mr. Eisenhower would have been acutely unhappy with Mr. Kennedy's presidential way of life. Probably the important question is not, What was this man's style as President? but rather, How well did this man carry out the duties that the American people entrust to the President?

Some of the people around President Kennedy felt that he did too much. They were concerned that his schedule was too full, that his working day was too long, that he did too many things himself that should have been done for him by assistants. This idea was emphasized by many news reporters in late spring, 1961, when it became known that Mr. Kennedy had suffered a back injury in a tree-planting ceremony in Canada. This trip was shortly followed by his European meetings with Premier Khrushchev, General de Gaulle, and Prime Minister Macmillan. On his return to the United States President Kennedy had to use crutches because of back pains. This dramatized the fact that he was pushing himself beyond safe limits.

Much space in the press was given to the nature of President Kennedy's schedule. It became clear that his daily program was too full for his physical health. Writers pointed out that no other President had permitted himself to take on quite so much. They urged him to slow down.

One journalist criticized the "nonsensical exertions which have come to be demanded of any President to support an absurd legend that he is just one of the boys." We have gotten into the habit, said this writer, "of treating our Presidents not only as public leaders but also as public utilities, on public call more or less like street cars." Said this same writer, "Nobody expects a corporation executive, a lawyer, or even a labor leader to drop everything and rush off to some chicken croquette luncheon to address the Master Barbers Association. Nobody supposes that such a man's value is measured so much by physical movement as by the exercise of his mind. Why should any President of the United States be put in lesser regard—particularly since the 40-hour week has never been extended to that office?"

Woodrow Wilson once cautioned the nation against killing its Presidents with overwork. Men of ordinary physique, he warned, "cannot be Presidents and live, if the strain be not somehow relieved. We shall be obliged always to be picking our Presidents from among wise and prudent athletes. . . ."

How did Mr. Kennedy spend his day? Like most of his predecessors, except that he packed more into each twenty-four-hour cycle. There were first of all the newspapers. Mr.

Kennedy regularly read half a dozen leading papers even before he appeared at his office at 9 or 9:30 in the morning. Then came the callers—Congressmen, Cabinet members, assistants and aides, advisers and consultants, foreign visitors of all degrees of importance from heads of state on down. Politicians and wire pullers, big and little, came too. There were lots of plain citizens as well, perhaps cashing in a promise that one day the President would see them. Every now and then a high school class, or the Boy Scouts, or a group of foreign students, or the child model for the Heart Fund drive got in to see him, too.

Luncheon was frequently a conference with lawmakers or advisers or assistants or important citizens—newspaper publishers, businessmen, labor leaders, personalities from the arts. A short rest was followed by a continuation of meetings, visits, the reading of reports. Mr. Kennedy managed to do a great deal of such reading. Those closest to him, including the White House correspondents, noted again and again that Mr. Kennedy was usually up on his facts. A *New York Times* reporter who watched the President at close range, commented: "Perhaps the White House's most voracious reader since Teddy Roosevelt, President Kennedy daily digests a dry mountain of reports, documents and top secret cables. He also scans American and foreign newspapers, news magazines and scholarly works on history and current affairs." He studied many of the official documents at night, after most of Washington had gone to bed.

Some days were broken up by official trips. Occasionally recreation—golf or swimming, usually—had a place in the day's routine. There were also endless parades, innumerable luncheons and dinners. However festive such meals might appear, they were seldom fun. Most men in public life regard such dining-out as chores to be endured, as obligations that accompany the job.

There were many ceremonial activities—the laying of wreaths, the dedication of buildings, highways, ships, and dams. Then there were the speeches. The President is called upon to speak at a huge variety of events. He accepts a small number. Sometimes he goes because he can't turn down a friend. Sometimes it's a political dinner designed to bail out his party from financial trouble. Sometimes it's an important college dedication or a charitable project. Sometimes he may want to take sides publicly on an important issue. By appearing in person at a certain event, he may give a strong boost to a social or humanitarian cause.

The President may welcome a particular opportunity to make a speech on a timely topic. He may decide to use a university setting to make a statement of international importance.

The President has a broad choice of media for communicating with the American people and with the world. Besides appearing in public, he may go on television and radio. Franklin Roosevelt invented the Fireside Chat so he could talk by radio to the American people in their homes. He created the illusion of the family gathered at the fireplace, sharing problems of common interest. People were ready to listen to him because they understood his words. His easy voice and manner attracted a big audience. This gave him political power that was respectfully noticed in Congress, especially.

One of the most common means of presidential communication is the press conference, which goes back to the early 1900's. Theodore Roosevelt, who relished big headlines about himself, made the first attempt to feed news regularly to the press. He had a number of friends in the business and he frequently gave them material for publication. Other journalists were unhappy at being excluded from the privileged circle but they could do nothing about it. There were no rules to which they could turn.

Woodrow Wilson, who became President in 1913, conducted the first true press conference, meeting all reporters on a basis of equality. He received oral questions and answered them on the spot. His successor, Warren G. Harding, got into trouble this way because he didn't know the answers. He then insisted on written questions, submitted in advance. This policy was adopted by Presidents Coolidge and Hoover, both of whom disliked press conferences.

When Franklin Roosevelt became President in 1933, he eliminated the written questions, and restored the form established by Woodrow Wilson. FDR delighted in the give-and-take of unrehearsed, unpredictable discussion. The conferences were thrown open to all writers who were approved by the correspondents' own association.

Presidents Truman and Eisenhower, before they faced the press, were briefed by their own staff. The idea was to prepare the President for all possible questions, to give him the facts before the reporters started demanding answers.

Under President Eisenhower the weekly press conference was televised, a practice continued by President Kennedy. Steadily the conference grew in size, until approximately four hundred correspondents began to appear. With such large numbers it was difficult to preserve an informal arrangement. Some writers complained that under Mr. Kennedy the conference was both rigid and uninformative. They felt it was not really illuminating but had become a series of elaborate announcements.

Some critics even felt that the press conference had outlived its usefulness. National and international affairs, they said, had become so delicate and yet so important, that they should not be debated at a sprawling press conference, where, as one journalist said, the President must endure "the ultimate cruelty of thinking aloud under pressure." These writers complained that the press conference touched on too many subjects too briefly—possibly twenty-five or thirty items in as little as half an hour. Instead, said these writers, the President should from time to time talk to the nation on radio and television and explain, slowly and in detail, some of the things he was thinking and doing. The American people needed a more leisurely but fuller explanation of the complicated problems facing the nation.

One long-experienced writer, Walter Lippmann, had this to say about the press conference of Mr. Kennedy:

> The President makes announcements and the correspondents ask him questions in order to get stories, perhaps even scoops. That is, I believe, a basically false conception of why it is worthwhile to have the President submit himself to questions from the press. The real use of the presidential press conference is to enable the President to explain his policies and, if necessary, to compel him to explain them.

Another journalist was more blunt. He said:

> The presidential news conference today is disorderly, disorganized, and hard on the lower back. With the television monsters all around, the reporters have become little more than props. One of our colleagues has compared the performance to making love in Carnegie Hall.

In spite of grumbling and dissatisfaction, many newspapermen, radio- and TV-men were not ready to see the press conference discontinued. When Mr. Kennedy skipped several sessions, as all Presidents have done, the complaints were louder than ever.

The President has other devices, too, by which he can reach the nation. He may, if he wishes, release information through his press secretary or through the unidentified "White House spokesman." This was an invention of President Calvin Coolidge who was sometimes willing to release information provided he was not named as the source. The reporters were obliged to give credit only to the "White House spokesman."

The important thing is that a major responsibility of the President is communication—with his people, with Congress, with the leaders and the people of other nations. In this generation no President can function successfully if he lacks this talent. Communication is a primary responsibility of his office, one that he cannot delegate to others. The ability to reach people, to explain to them so they understand, is one of the fine arts of this office.

One more thing should be said. When the President does speak, the nation and the world listen. This is a special quality of the job. The President of the United States, head of the most powerful free nation in the world, has a ready audience no matter what he says. This gives him a big natural advantage.

Woodrow Wilson, long before he entered the White House, summed up the President's role as Voice of the Nation. Once the President has won the country's confidence, said Mr. Wilson,

> . . . no other single force can withstand him, no combination of forces will easily overpower him. His position takes the imagination of the country. He is the representative of no constituency, but of the whole people. When he speaks in his true character, he speaks for no special interest. If he rightly interpret the national thought and boldly insist upon it, he is irresistible. . . .

★   ★

Chapter Nine

THE MAN IN THE OVAL OFFICE

The President of the United States plays a variety of important roles. His powers, as enumerated in the Constitution, merely hint at the work of this office. To get a picture of the job it is necessary to study the living Presidency, to see how the Chief Executive actually uses his power.

What are some responsibilities that—written or unwritten —belong to the man who sits in the great oval office in the White House?

To begin with he is expected to take the lead in proposing needed laws and then to follow through and see that the laws are passed. The Constitution says that the President shall "recommend" to Congress "such measures as he shall judge necessary." But custom dictates that he go much further.

Some Presidents, especially in earlier years, have had little to do with the lawmaking process. Presidents Franklin Pierce, James Buchanan, Ulysses Grant, Benjamin Harrison, William H. Taft, and Calvin Coolidge believed that their function was defined in the title, "Chief Executive." They took their lead from the line in the Constitution directing the President to "take care that the laws be faithfully executed. . . ." They saw little need to formulate laws or guide them through Congress.

A few recent Presidents, especially in their early days in office, have tried to let Congress handle the business of lawmaking. Mr. Truman and Mr. Eisenhower, for example, started out on the assumption that legislation was the special preserve of Congress. These Chief Executives hoped that the lawmakers would do the right thing by the President and enact the laws that the President felt were desirable. Both men worked hard to promote friendship between the White House and Capitol Hill, where laws are made. Both were disappointed to learn that friendly relations with congressmen did not guarantee the passage of laws the President wanted. Like many another President, they learned that if they expected their favored laws to pass, they would have to get busy personally. They also learned there was only one way to block legislation they did not want—by intervening with all their strength.

Some Presidents have happily embraced the chance to work for their own legislative program and to oppose laws they considered bad.

Theodore Roosevelt, Woodrow Wilson, Franklin Roosevelt, and John Kennedy are among the American Presidents who entered deeply into lawmaking. Franklin Roosevelt went so far as to label some of his proposals "must" legislation. In the early years of his Presidency, Congress was willing to grant him what he asked. The nation at the time was deep in trouble, with industry paralyzed and the hungry unemployed crying for help. Congress was glad to follow the President's leadership in this crisis. After a few years, however, the lawmakers grew balky and finally rejected the idea of receiving "must" legislation from the Chief Executive.

How does the President get involved in the lawmaking

process? Sometimes by starting the legislative ball rolling himself. Many laws have had their beginning right in the President's office. His Cabinet, his assistants and advisers, his friends in Congress, his party leaders all over the nation —and he, personally—may come up with ideas. If the President favors a particular law, he may actually help to write it or he may make general suggestions and turn the writing job over to assistants. He calls on his supporters in both houses of Congress to get behind it and push. They must be alert not only to enemies who would kill the bill but to others who would smother it with amendments. Party leaders in Congress steer the law through the treacherous byways it must follow from its first introduction to final passage.

If the President strongly wants a law passed, he may take personal command of the campaign. He seeks the support of friendly party members, of course. But he goes much further and tries to corral members of the opposition party as well. How does he do this? By a variety of ways. One is to invite them to the White House for breakfast—or maybe lunch or dinner—to talk things over. He may entertain them in ones, twos, threes or more, depending on conditions. This friendly approach may be effective with some congressmen and not with others. The President tries to use the tactics that will bring each member of Congress around.

In the summer of 1961 President and Mrs. Kennedy gave an unprecedented dinner at George Washington's Mt. Vernon estate to honor the visiting President of Pakistan. Among the limited number of fortunate guests were a couple of congressmen who were known enemies of the President's foreign aid bill, then being debated in Congress. Some keen observers quickly figured out why the congressmen had been asked to this sparkling social event.

Somewhere in his talks with congressmen, the President may use his power of patronage—the handing out of Federal jobs. Many a congressman has been persuaded to support a

Presidential bill in return for patronage plums. Every politician has responsibilities to his followers. The more jobs he can offer them, the stronger their support is likely to be. While some students of government deplore this use of patronage by the President, others point out that all governments—in all countries and in all periods of history—have dispensed jobs in exchange for support.

Not every congressman can be enticed with the promise of jobs for his supporters back home. Some lawmakers are more interested in having a Federal building project go into their state or district—say a post office or a new harbor or a Federal bridge or dam. If the President is agreeable to this, the congressman may in turn become enthusiastic about the particular law the President wants.

Still other congressmen may be impressed by the threat that when they next run for office they will get no support from the White House. This may also mean that they will have to manage without money or speakers from the national committee. Congressmen know that the President can have a lot to say about the distribution of party funds and party talent. Few men would want to campaign without some official support from the President and the party leaders.

The President may do lots of other things, too, in the course of making a bill into law. He may go on radio and television to get the people to support his legislative ideas. If he is a skillful persuader, he may stimulate the public to bring pressure on their congressmen in his favor. He may build a fire under members of Congress and force them to move his way.

This ability to trigger public action is a special quality. Probably no President had it quite in the way of FDR. He sensed when to go on the air, what to say, and how to say it for the results he needed. But the President must use his talents economically. To make too many public appeals is dangerous. He must not allow himself to become "over-

exposed" if he wants to speak with strong effect. The fact
nevertheless remains that any President—even one who is not
a great TV talent—commands a big audience just because he
is President. Many a congressman has been sobered by the
mail that may follow a presidential talk. And when the people
speak, a congressman listens.

Occasionally, in a critical case, the President may telephone a congressman to ask his support. Most members of
Congress are flattered by such attention, though a few may
regard it as an unwelcome intrusion into the lawmaker's
domain.

Many congressmen have had visits or phone calls from
Cabinet members or officials in the President's Executive
Office. "The President wants . . ." is the spoken or unspoken
message. Members of the President's official family make
such calls and visits to help the President win votes for his
bills. This is generally considered part of the President's
legislative responsibility.

Some writers have criticized the President for bringing
pressure on members of Congress. According to these writers,
the President has no business going after congressional votes
and support. He is the executive, Congress is the legislative,
and they should operate independently. The President should
neither cultivate them nor tempt them nor threaten them, say
these critics. But every student of history—and every President—knows that there is another criticism that is even
worse. This is the charge that the President did nothing to
get his ideas enacted into law; that he walked away from
his responsibility; that he did not press for passage of a bill
he wanted; and that the bill therefore went down to defeat.

The President's legislative duties occupy only a scant
line in the Constitution. But they nevertheless absorb much
of his time and energy. Similarly, many of the other things
he does are not detailed in the Constitution. We have already
referred to Article II, Section 3 of the Constitution which

says that the President "shall take care that the laws be faithfully executed. . . ." This is a broad grant of power, and it is up to the President to determine what to do and how to do it.

Nowhere, for example, is the President officially declared to be leader of his party. Yet the practice for many years has been that the President is party chief. This makes some people uncomfortable. They feel that the President should be above party; that his dignity and stature demand that he be free of any political involvements. But this is an unrealistic view of the Presidency. The fact is that party leadership is an inescapable presidential responsibility, as important as any enumerated in the Constitution.

A President with talent as a party leader is a stronger Chief Executive. The power of party leadership gives him a better chance to get his program through Congress; to influence the election of congressmen sympathetic to his goals; to reach into the states and districts to the voters themselves for understanding and support.

The President, of course, is leader of all the American people, not just of his party. It is a remarkable fact that almost all Presidents have successfully bridged this gap and functioned as Chief Executive of the whole nation as well as of their party.

One of the criticisms often made about democracy is that it is inefficient; that it cannot mobilize its strength even in a crisis; that every proposal for national action may be smothered in talk. Effective party leadership by the President is a corrective to this weakness. As head of his party, the President can demand that certain things be done. He can reward party members who go along and punish those who don't. He can insist on enough discipline so that the party, at least, will show up creditably. Only the President can provide such leadership in our democracy. Only the President can prevent the disaster that has overtaken some other democracies—indecision, endless and inconclusive debate, and final paralysis. The President's power as party leader is a weapon in the service of the nation itself.

This does not mean, of course, that the President should become personally embroiled in local political squabbles. But it does mean that he should help to decide the policies and philosophy of his party; that he should be consulted about the men of his party who will run for the United States Senate, the House of Representatives, state governorships, and even some important local offices.

Most Presidents have decided who should head the party's national committee, what candidates for high office it should back, and with how much money. Occasionally Presidents have staked their own prestige on particular candidates by publicly supporting them and even making a speaking tour on their behalf. This does not always succeed. A candidate may go down in spite of a presidential blessing. Such a defeat doesn't help the President of course. But everybody expects him to continue leading the party just the same.

The President controls the party's nominating machinery. Once in office he is sure to win the party's nomination a second time. While he is limited to two terms by the Twenty-second Amendment, enacted in 1951, he can sometimes name his successor if he wants to. Most Presidents, understandably, wish to see their policies continued and will have this in mind when choosing from the available candidates.

The party needs the President as much as the President needs the party. For one thing political parties are almost always in the red. But the party whose man is in the White House has a sure way of climbing out of its financial hole. This is the big fund-raising dinner at which the President himself is the chief speaker. Faithful party members, always ready to rally round the President, produce the funds that are needed for future operations.

The party that is not in power lacks this primary drawing

card. It has to settle for perhaps an ex-President or two or other leaders below presidential rank.

Another of the President's major duties—the first one cited in the Constitution—is "Commander-in-chief of the Army and Navy." This was included to make it forever clear that our armed forces were to be under civilian, not military, control. Active leadership of the various branches is, of course, entrusted to professional fighting men. But the highest responsible official is the elected President. The final decision of when to employ the armed forces and how to employ them must, by law, be made by the President himself.

The Constitution gives to Congress the right to declare war. Officially, therefore, the United States cannot wage war with another country until Congress has made an appropriate declaration. But actually it is the President who holds the war-making power. As Commander-in-Chief of the armed forces, he can dispatch them or withhold them at will. As chief officer for conducting the nation's foreign relations, he can promote peace or he can make war unavoidable. This is true even though the Constitution requires him to share certain foreign relations duties with the Senate—the making of treaties and the appointing of ambassadors.

President Theodore Roosevelt, using United States warships, helped Panama revolt against Colombia. In fact he later said, "I took the Canal Zone and let Congress debate, and while the debate goes on the Canal does also." President Coolidge sent United States Marines into Nicaragua in 1927 to put down revolution and protect American investments. In 1940 President Franklin Roosevelt swapped fifty naval destroyers for some island bases belonging to Great Britain. This act appeared necessary to the President to save Britain from annihilation by the Nazis. To Hitler it appeared as an act of war and he said so.

In 1950 President Truman, alarmed by communist North

Korea's surprise attack on South Korea, sent United States forces to stop the invaders. The United Nations then took up the cause and assumed command of the campaign to drive back the aggressors. But United States fighting men had moved first, on presidential order.

These examples show that while the "declaration" of war may still be Congress' responsibility, the President has the real power to wage war—and has done so—without an official declaration. The declaration has often followed the start of actual fighting.

This does not suggest that the President takes this responsibility lightly. Before any United States President sends armed forces into action he weighs the choices carefully. Once the Red forces began to pour into South Korea in 1950, Mr. Truman knew that within days there would be no South Korea left to defend. He had to act promptly or see South Korea disappear as an independent, non-communist country. Most Americans applauded his act as correct —and brave.

Every President realizes, of course, the seriousness of any move he makes in the foreign relations field. Frequently, before he decides on action, he calls in leaders from the opposition party to ask their understanding and support. From time to time the President in office consults the former President or Presidents to gain their counsel and to give a non-political, non-partisan quality to the action he takes. Usually he also consults and informs the leaders of other nations with whom the United States is allied.

Since the 1930's the President of the United States has been the recognized spokesman for the democracies. As the resources of the United States were thrown into the war against the Nazis, the nations turned to the United States for leadership. During World War II the heart of strategy was located in Washington. After the war, only the United States was prepared and willing to lend a hand to the war-ravaged countries.

Through the Marshall Plan and the Point Four program of President Truman, the United States proved that its friendship was as strong in peace as in war.

As it became clear that the Soviet Union had other, conflicting aims, the non-communist nations moved closer to the United States. In the postwar period, the United States acted vigorously to stop the aggressive march of communism. It posted the Truman Doctrine in Greece and Turkey, helped fashion NATO as a shield for western, non-communist governments of Europe, put forth the Eisenhower Doctrine for the Middle East, and tried in the UN to assure the safety of the non-communist countries.

Starting with the close of World War II, the United States backed up its words about peace and friendship with about seventy billion dollars in grants and loans. These funds, requested by the President and voted by Congress, were poured into the faltering economies of many nations. It was hoped that this assistance, both military and non-military, would help these nations first of all hold on to life, and then fight their way to economic health.

This vast program made the United States a headquarters for the non-communist nations of the world. It made the President of the United States a key person for many people outside the United States. His words, his acts had effects way beyond the shores of his own country. The United States program for foreign aid gave the President new prestige—and great new burdens.

Matching the President's broader responsibilities in the world were added tasks at home. By the Employment Act of 1946, the President must watch over the nation's economic condition. The Act gives him able assistants, but as in everything else he does, he is held accountable. If, during his term in office, the nation should suffer economic depression and unemployment, he would be expected to act promptly to bring relief. If his program failed, he and his party would surely be defeated at the next election. The American voter can be counted on to blame the party in power for economic troubles and to elect their opponents at the first chance.

The President has many other duties—some enumerated, some not—to fill his day. While the Constitution mentions some important jobs the President is required to fill, it does not suggest that he shall be a grand dispenser of patronage. Yet this chore can consume much presidential time. Every President has been plagued by the problem of job seekers. This is true even though we have a merit system, with competitive examinations for almost all government employment. That still leaves many positions to be filled by the President.

The handing out of jobs is not altogether unwelcome to the President. He naturally wants to reward his friends, especially those who worked for him before he won the nomination. But no President enjoys being dogged by candidates hungry for work in government. Abraham Lincoln complained bitterly about the time he was forced to spend with these people. President Garfield was shot by a man who felt he deserved a government appointment. President Eisenhower was dismayed by the stubborn insistence of office-hungry Republicans. Like many another President, John Kennedy delegated most patronage work to a trusted staff. They screened applicants and saw that, whenever possible, job priorities went to (1) sound Democrats, (2) early Kennedy supporters, (3) qualified workers.

Patronage is a thankless business. President Taft once said that for every appointment he made he created "nine enemies and one ingrate." When Charles Evans Hughes ran for President in 1916, Republican campaign workers were glum about their job prospects. They circulated a story that when Hughes was governor of New York, a supporter had come to him for a job and been turned down. "I cannot have it said," Hughes is supposed to have remarked, "that I have distributed offices as a reward for support." Some of Hughes' workers felt that their prospects were grim, whether Hughes won or lost. They feared that the harder they toiled the more certain it was they would be denied jobs.

Chief Executives know, of course, that patronage is a source of strength to them as well as a robber of time and energy. Many a legislative bill needed by the President, as already explained, has become law because the President distributed the right amount of patronage in the right places.

Few Presidents would agree publicly with Senator William Marcy of New York, who in 1831 explained the uses of the patronage or spoils system. Referring to his friends, powerful political chieftains in New York, Marcy admitted that they "are not so fastidious as some gentlemen are, as to disclosing the principles on which they act. They boldly preach what they practice. When they are contending for victory, they avow their intention of enjoying the fruits of it. If they are defeated, they expect to retire from office. If they are successful, they claim, as a matter of right, the advantages of success. They see nothing wrong in the rule that to the victor belong the spoils of the enemy."

With a change in administration, about four thousand jobs become available to the President. They range from Cabinet posts and high ambassadorships to postmasterships around the country. Obviously the task of sorting out candidates for these appointments is delicate business. The President wants to reward the right people, he wants to see capable workers fill these jobs, and he wants to cooperate with the United States Senator in whose state the prospective jobholder lives.

For many years United States senators have enjoyed the privilege of passing judgment on job applicants from their state. If a particular candidate is objectionable to the senator, his name is dropped. This power of United States senators is known as "senatorial courtesy." No President tries to force a nomination if it is contrary to a senator's wish, because all senators stand together on these matters. They would simply refuse to confirm such an appointment.

With the Presidency goes a full crop of annoyances and

frustrations. The President's official family is so big that at any time some individual member may say or do something that will make trouble for the Chief. It is almost inevitable that from time to time such episodes will hit the front pages. In the Truman government some high Democratic officials were publicly disgraced when it became known that they had thrown favors to some bankers and businessmen and had received costly gifts in return. During Dwight Eisenhower's administration, Presidential Assistant Sherman Adams was forced out of office by evidence that he had improperly accepted gifts and performed services for a businessman friend.

One of the first disillusionments that came to John F. Kennedy after his inauguration in 1961 was the realization that secrets have a way of leaking out. Like every President before him, he was chagrined and irritated to learn that confidential information can become public knowledge with amazing speed. Then, very early in his Presidency, Mr. Kennedy learned that comments by his assistants can embarrass the administration. One of his high officials was quoted in the press as criticizing the administration's limited achievements to date. The man was reported to have said, "At this point we are like the Harlem Globetrotters, passing forward, behind, sidewise and underneath. But nobody has made a basket yet." Pounced on by his colleagues in and around the White House, the harried official denied having made the statement and explained, "My position is that this Administration is scoring a basket every thirty seconds by the clock." Some people thought the explanation was worse than the original slip.

When the Russians launched their Sputnik in 1957, Eisenhower's Presidential Assistant Sherman Adams unfortunately labeled it just a shot in "outer space basketball." And Charles Wilson, who had just resigned as Eisenhower's Secretary of Defense, didn't help matters by his judgment of Sputnik.

"Why worry?" he asked. "It isn't going to fall down and hit you on the head, you know."

Early in the Kennedy administration, on April 12, 1961, the Russian Yuri Gagarin was lofted into space. Excited reporters phoned the chief of the United States astronautical Project Mercury for a comment on the epic event. Awakened from his early morning sleep, the Air Force Lieutenant Colonel gave a reply that shook the White House: "If you want anything from us, you jerk, the answer is that we are all asleep."

Another irritant to Presidents is the long time it takes before their orders are put into effect. There is a common belief that a President needs only to ask for something and that action will follow. The fact is that below the President stands a huge bureaucracy, the tens of thousands of government officials and workers who carry on the day-by-day work of administration. A presidential order may be passed down the line, but as many a President has learned, it may take a long time before anything happens. This is not necessarily because the staff want to frustrate the President. But government machinery is ponderous and slow moving; sometimes an order gets lost in the labyrinth of government agencies.

Franklin D. Roosevelt, who served longer than any other President, wrote from experience about getting things done:

> The Treasury is so large and far-flung and ingrained in its practices that I find it almost impossible to get the action and results I want. . . . But the Treasury is not to be compared with the State Department. You should go through the experience of trying to get any changes in the thinking, policy and action of the career diplomats and then you'd know what a real problem was. But the Treasury and the State Department put together are nothing compared with the Na-a-vy. The admirals are really something to cope with—and I should know. To change anything in the Na-a-vy is like punching a

feather bed. You punch it with your right and you punch it with your left until you are finally exhausted, and then you find the damn bed just as it was before you started punching.

The disappointments, the irritations, and the blunders that harass the President are many. How does he find relief? By occasional sport or vacations or rest. But even when the President goes off duty, he carries his burdens with him. No matter where he is, he remains on call. On his "vacation" cruises, President Franklin Roosevelt regularly received his mail, laws to be signed, official documents to be approved, and a big assortment of paper work that he called the "morning's wash."

Though the President is on duty around the clock, his occasional trips or golf may draw unfriendly comment from some newspapers and some citizens. While everybody knows the President has too much to do, his efforts to relax seem to surprise some people.

The President is denied the right of privacy. He lives at the best-known address in the world, a national focus of interest. During the Kennedy administration, record crowds, averaging more than a million a year, lined up to see a part, at least, of their President's home. When Mrs. Kennedy announced that she would redecorate the interior and furnish it with American antiques, public curiosity about the presidential mansion became greatly intensified.

Few ordinary citizens get to see the President or his family on these tours, because the upper floors, where they live, are closed to visitors. But the regular business of the Presidency and the steady stream of official guests, domestic and foreign, bring much traffic through the White House. In addition, the presidential receptions, small and large, make necessary a great amount of coming and going in the President's home.

In the fall of 1961 the Kennedys had as White House guests former President and Mrs. Truman. The visit coincided with news from Russia that Premier Khrushchev had just had

Stalin's body removed from its place of honor in Moscow's Red Square. Said President Kennedy: "Don't say there's no justice in the world. Stalin has been kicked out of Lenin's tomb and President Truman is back in the White House."

Most Presidents have maintained other residences outside Washington during their term of office so that occasionally, at least, they could drop their official cares. This is especially important in recent times, as the tempo of world events has been stepped up. President Theodore Roosevelt could comfortably accommodate his six active children in the White House. But President John F. Kennedy, when he hunted for a house in nearby Virginia, explained, "I think it's good for young children to get out of the governmental atmosphere."

Once in office, Presidents have tended to limit sharply their social contact with former friends and colleagues. This is not unusual among executives occupying lofty positions. To some extent it's a result of the isolation that goes with living at the summit. When President Hoover received President-elect Roosevelt before the 1933 inauguration, Mr. Roosevelt commented that the President would probably be too busy to return the call. Replied President Hoover: "Mr. Roosevelt, you'll learn pretty soon that the President of the United States doesn't call on anybody."

Again and again the question is asked, Why, if the Presidency is such a lonely job, such a tough job, so full of troubles and sacrifice, does anybody want it? The answer is that some men do not shrink from hard work, even cruelly hard work. A certain type of personality is lured by the excitement and the opportunity of massive responsibility. The rewards, as they see it, are mighty—the distinction of joining that small group of men who have won immortality by writing the history of the world's most important free nation. The Presidents and the presidential aspirants have thought the sacrifice minor compared to the satisfactions.

President Harry Truman, who enjoyed being President,

once said with typical frankness, "There are probably a million people in this country who could do the presidential job better than I, but I've got the job and I'm doing the very best I can."

Mr. Truman when he inherited the Presidency on Franklin Roosevelt's death, was rated low by some experts. He just would not measure up, they said. But Harry Truman proved again that it is possible for an intelligent, honest, courageous, and devoted American to fill the most responsible and demanding job in the land. In the long run, these qualities—intelligence, honesty, courage, and devotion to American ideals—have characterized our Chief Executives. In some cases it was not clear until a man actually became President that he had these qualities, but once in office, most of our Presidents have shown these virtues in impressive degree.

Abraham Lincoln, on his inauguration, described his fifteen predecessors in the White House. The Presidents have led the nation, said Lincoln, "through many perils, and generally with great success." What Abraham Lincoln said of the Presidents in 1861 remains true a century later.

GLOSSARY

Availability. This is a term used by politicians to describe a candidate who, in their judgment, has a good chance of winning the Presidency. Many qualities go into this judgment. A candidate who has a strong array of these characteristics is "available," and will get the serious consideration of party leaders.

Boss. A political leader who wields great power in his party. He may operate on the ward level or on the state or national level. Some experts think he's a dying species, that a more intelligent group of voters are replacing him with more representative, democratic-minded leaders.

Brain Trust. This term was applied to the group of men who helped Franklin Roosevelt put together the New Deal in the early period of his Presidency. The Brain Trust included a number of professors and scholars. Some criticism was stirred by the unusual sight of intellectuals close to the President.

Caucus. A private, unofficial meeting held by members of a political party to decide, for example, on policies or on a candidate.

Civil rights. This refers to the rights of minorities, especially Negroes, to enjoy the full benefits of our democratic nation. It relates chiefly to their right to vote freely, to attend the public schools and to use all public facilities including trains, buses, waiting rooms and restaurants free of any discrimination. It refers also to their right to higher education, to housing of their choice and to jobs on a basis of equality with whites.

Communism. This economic system was devised by the German philosopher, Karl Marx, who claimed it alone could solve the great problems of our age: war, poverty, unemployment, ignorance, crime and extremes of wealth. Marx asked that the government take over the ownership and operation of all businesses; that private individuals lose the right to make profit from their own enterprises. According to Marx, these changes would be followed by a Utopian order in which all people would enjoy the good life. His theories have never taken hold in the United States, where private enterprise has been the heart of our economic system. Both major parties in the United States supported the idea that the private enterprise system must be under government regulation. The parties differ, however, as to how much supervision the government should have.

Conservative. This word describes someone who believes in free, private enterprise, where each man makes his own way. Conservatives usually oppose laws that increase government benefits to workers, that provide higher social security payments, public low-cost housing, federal aid to education and federal health programs. These activities, conservatives feel, are costly; they result in higher taxes and finally lead to socialism or communism.

Dark horse. This is a presidential aspirant who is not believed to be in the running, but who may be named by his party convention under special conditions. This can happen when a convention is deadlocked, with the leading figures unwilling to yield. Then a dark horse may stand a chance of capturing the nomination.

Draft. This is a movement designed to place the wreath of presidential nominee on someone who is supposedly not in the race. Back of the draft is the theory that the office should seek the man and not the other way round. Many would-be candidates would like it to appear that they were drafted. Most seasoned political workers believe a real draft is close to impossible, that most drafts are phony.

Egghead. A term of derision that was much used beginning in the campaign of 1952. Adlai Stevenson, Democratic presidential candidate, attracted many intellectuals into his camp. He and they were both described as dreamers whose heads were in the political clouds.

Eisenhower doctrine. This was presented to Congress in 1957 by President Eisenhower who was worried by Russian aggression in the Middle East. It authorized the President to use economic and military means to block communist expansion in the area.

Electoral college. Every state, and beginning in 1964 the District of Columbia, is entitled to a certain number of presidential electors. In the case of each state, this number is the total of the state's membership in both houses of Congress. The District of Columbia has been allotted three electors. To win the Presidency a candidate must get a majority of votes in the electoral college. Electors meet in their separate state capitals to cast their ballots for President and Vice President.

Fair Deal. This was President Harry Truman's name for his program to promote the economic and social health of the nation.

Favorite son. A term that describes a presidential hopeful whose strength is limited, usually, to his own state. He stands but a slight chance of winning the nomination. In the case of a tie among prominent candidates, a favorite son might be brought forward. Generally the favorite son has to be content to get a short-lived puff in the form of a courtesy nomination, and then fade from view.

Federal system. This was the balance created between the national government and the states. All the states were bound together under a federal government called the United States of America. At the same time each state retained a good deal of independence.

Founding Fathers. This refers to the men who gathered in 1787 to write the Constitution. Included in the group were George Washington, Alexander Hamilton, James Madison, John Jay, Benjamin Franklin.

Gerrymandering. By this process, the party in control of a state molds election districts in such a way that it will gain a majority of votes. Sometimes to encompass such a majority, a district is tortured into a weird shape. The district may protrude, curve or bend in odd ways to reach into certain areas, while avoiding others.

G.O.P. Since the 1880's the letters "G.O.P.," which stand for "Grand Old Party," have symbolized the Republican Party.

Kitchen cabinet. This term was applied in unfriendly criticism of President Jackson, who met informally with friends. The implication was that the President was getting advice from unauthorized and unofficial persons. There is nothing in the Constitution to limit the President's right to seek help wherever he chooses.

Liberal. This term is applied to people who believe the government should step in to protect the rights of workers, the poor, the slum dwellers, the unemployed. Liberals believe these groups cannot match the power of the business-owning class unless the government assumes certain responsibilities. See New Deal for additional detail on liberalism.

Machine. As used in politics, this word means a political organization. All parties have their machines. Some are well organized and efficient, some are not. Party machinery exists in the local area, the county, the state and the nation. In a presidential election, each party strives to perfect its machine, from the local district on up to the national organization.

Madison Avenue sell. The heart of America's advertising industry is Madison Avenue, New York City. The street has come to symbolize high-pressure advertising—extravagant claims, a highly polished surface, a lack of sincerity.

Majority. More than half. In politics this may mean as little as one vote more than 50 per cent.

Marshall Plan. This was originally proposed in a 1947 speech by Truman's Secretary of State, George Marshall. Eventually it became a giant operation in which United States funds were used to bring to life the war-beaten European nations. Many countries took advantage of this opportunity to start up their industries and get their people back to work. The results of the Marshall Plan more than justified the original hopes for it.

Merit system. This was developed to curb the abuses of the spoils system. Under the merit system, many government jobs were made subject to competitive examination. A Civil Service was organized to supervise the operation and assure that jobs were distributed on the basis of merit rather than political favoritism.

Minority Party. See Third Party.

National chairman. He is usually designated by the President, but elected by the party's national committee. The breadth and quality of his power depend on the President. Some chairmen have had a dominant position in the party; others have been executives with limited power.

National committee. Each major party has a national committee consisting of a man and woman from each state, the District of Columbia, Puerto Rico and, for the Democratic Party, from the Virgin Islands and the Canal Zone. This committee selects the national chairman and helps him run the party.

National nominating convention. This is held every four years by each major party to name its presidential candidate. Delegates to the convention are named by the state party organization. The convention is organized and managed by the national committee of each party. Following the convention the campaign begins.

New Deal. This label was given to the social and welfare program of President Franklin Roosevelt, especially in his first two terms— 1933 to 1940. The New Deal included such ideas as old-age pensions, unemployment insurance, low-cost public housing, minimum-wage and maximum-hour laws and encouragement of labor unions. These proposals were happily received by industrial workers, city dwellers and "liberals," and were opposed by many farmers, the owners of businesses and factories and other "conservatives."

New Freedom. This was President Woodrow Wilson's term for his program. It included strong efforts to bring business under government control and to spread the benefits of our economic system to the poorer classes.

New Frontier. President-elect John F. Kennedy promised his best efforts to improve the condition not only of the American people but of the world. Peace and economic health for all nations were his goal. For this aim he asked for support—and even sacrifice—by the American people.

Patronage. This is the President's power to hand out jobs, beginning with the highest assignments in the national capital and in the foreign service. Patronage is a great source of presidential strength. Many Presidents have used patronage as a means of getting congressmen to support presidential bills.

Plurality. A number greater than any of the others. If, for example, there are several contestants, whoever gets the most votes has a plurality. This may be well below a majority of all the votes.

Point Four. This term came from the 1949 inaugural speech by President Truman. In it he offered to help other nations learn American technological methods. Many countries benefited from the assistance of American experts, scientists and technicians.

Senatorial courtesy. This is the unwritten right of a United States senator to pass judgment on a man from his state who is being considered by the President for appointment to a job. If the senator says No, the President will withdraw the applicant's name. It is well understood that the senators stand together in preserving this ancient privilege.

Popular vote. Voters go to the polls on presidential election day to cast their ballots for electors named by their party. These electors, it is assumed, will support the candidate named by the national party convention. The electors winning the greatest number of popular votes in the state are said to carry the state. The winners take all the electoral votes of the state; the losers get none. To capture the state's electoral vote requires only a plurality—rather than a majority—of popular votes.

Primary. This is an election designed to give the voters a chance to name the party's candidate for office. It was devised as a way of curbing the power of political bosses and giving it to the people instead.

Proportional representation. By such a plan, the competing parties in a state would win electors in proportion to their popular votes. Under our electoral system the party with the most popular votes wins all the electors of the state.

Public opinion poll. This is based on a sample of opinions held by different classes of people. The pollsters usually ask their questions of just a few thousand people. But these few thousand are carefully selected, so they contain the right proportions of poor, middle class and rich; factory workers, farmers, bankers, industrialists and housewives; the educated, the uneducated and the half-educated. The pollsters believe that if they sample the right proportions of people, they can tell what the country as a whole thinks of a candidate or an idea.

Ratification. The Constitution says that for an amendment to become law, it must be approved, or ratified, by three-fourths of the states.

Silk Stocking District. This is a wealthy voting district and may be expected, generally, to support Republican candidates.

Socialism. In general aim it resembles communism. It differs as to tactics and strategy. Like communism, it has had little popular acceptance in the United States. See Communism.

Social security laws. These measures include unemployment compensation, old age pensions and financial help to the handicapped. The New Deal of Franklin Roosevelt gave a big boost to the idea of social security in this country. The system has been steadily expanded and made more liberal.

Sovereignty. Independence. As related to the states and the national government, it means that the states yield certain powers—for example, taxation, foreign affairs, armed forces—but retain others such as education, marriage laws, police matters. In certain respects, therefore, the states remain sovereign. Their rights may not be curbed by the national government.

Spoils system. This is an ancient practice whereby the winner in a political contest rewards his friends with jobs, often at the expense of the defeated party.

Square Deal. This was devised by President Theodore Roosevelt as a way of regulating business to protect the nation as a whole. Businessmen were alarmed by what they feared was a hostile attitude of the President.

Third party. Since the beginning of American history, there have been small parties, also known as third parties, or splinter parties, that contested with the big ones at the polls. Though victory has always gone to one of the two major parties, the small parties have continued to try for public support. They have focused attention on issues and have sometimes seen their own ideas stolen by the big parties. Generally the small parties have had little popular support.

Totalitarian country. This is a nation under the rule of one man, usually, and under one party. The Soviet Union under Stalin and Khrushchev, Spain under Franco, are examples. The system is marked by the absence of basic freedoms—speech, press, assembly, voting. These nations are sometimes referred to as "police states" because government surveillance and power are total and oppressive.

Two-thirds rule. The Democratic convention, through most of its history, nominated its presidential candidates by a two-thirds majority. This was felt to be undemocratic and in 1936 the party changed its procedure to correspond to the Republican rule—a majority of delegates named the candidate.

Whistle stop. This refers to presidential campaigning from the rear platform of a train. At villages big and small, the people gather at the railroad stop to see and hear the presidential candidate. This is an informal but effective way of exhibiting a candidate. The whistle stop has to some extent been replaced by the airplane caravan.

SUGGESTED FURTHER READING

Bendiner, Robert, *White House Fever*, Harcourt, Brace, 1960.

Binkley, Wilfred E., *The Man in the White House*, John Hopkins Press, 1959.

Corwin, Edward S. and Koenig, Louis W., *The President Today*, New York University Press, 1956.

Fincher, Ernest B., *The President of the United States*, Abelard-Schuman, 1955.

Finer, Herman, *The Presidency: Crisis and Regeneration*, University of Chicago Press, 1960.

Hillman, William, *Mr. President*, Farrar, Straus and Young, 1952.

Hoyt, Edwin P., *Jumbos and Jackasses*, Doubleday & Company, 1960.

Hyman, Sidney, *The American President*, Harper and Brothers, 1954.

Laski, Harold J., *The American Presidency*, Harper and Brothers, 1940.

Lorant, Stephen, *The Presidency*, The Macmillan Company, 1951.

Neustadt, Richard, *Presidential Power*, John Wiley and Sons, Inc., 1960.

Pollard, James E., *The President and the Press*, The Macmillan Company, 1947.

Rossiter, Clinton, *The American Presidency*, Harcourt, Brace, 1960.

Weingast, David E., *Franklin D. Roosevelt: Man of Destiny*, Julian Messner, Inc., 1952.

White, Theodore H., *The Making of the President, 1960*, Atheneum, 1961.

Williams, Irving G., *The Rise of the Vice Presidency*, Public Affairs Press, 1956.

INDEX

185

About the Author

DAVID WEINGAST was born in Newark, New Jersey, and attended public schools there. He completed his undergraduate work at New York University, moving on to Columbia University for his Master's and Doctor of Philosophy degrees. The recipient of a Ford Foundation grant he spent 1953 and '54 in Europe doing political research. For many years he was a teacher of history, Chairman of the Social Studies Department in Newark high schools and lecturer in political science at Rutgers University. He is now Assistant Superintendent in charge of Newark high schools.